CULTURES OF THE WORLD

Benin

Cavendish
Square

New York

Published in 2021 by Cavendish Square Publishing, LLC
243 5th Avenue, Suite 136, New York, NY 10016
Copyright © 2021 by Cavendish Square Publishing, LLC

Third Edition

Website: cavendishsq.com

This publication represents the opinions and views of the author based on his or her personal experience, knowledge, and research. The information in this book serves as a general guide only. The author and publisher have used their best efforts in preparing this book and disclaim liability rising directly or indirectly from the use and application of this book.

All websites were available and accurate when this book was sent to press.

Library of Congress Cataloging-in-Publication Data

Names: Kneib, Martha, author. | Nevins, Debbie, author.
Title: Benin / Martha Kneib and Debbie Nevins.
Other titles: Cultures of the world.
Description: Third edition. | New York : Cavendish Square Publishing, 2021.
  | Series: Cultures of the world | Includes bibliographical references
  and index.
Identifiers: LCCN 2020049878 | ISBN 9781502662538 (library binding) | ISBN
  9781502662545 (ebook)
Subjects: LCSH: Benin--Juvenile literature.
Classification: LCC DT541.22 .K58 2021 | DDC 966.83--dc23
LC record available at https://lccn.loc.gov/2020049878

Writers: Martha Kneib; Debbie Nevins, third edition
Editor, third edition: Debbie Nevins
Designer, third edition: Jessica Nevins
Picture Researcher, third edition: Jessica Nevins

Find us on

CONTENTS

BENIN TODAY

BENIN IS A SMALL COUNTRY ON THE VAST CONTINENT OF AFRICA. Located on the Atlantic Ocean along the southern coast of West Africa, it is a land of great natural and human diversity. It encompasses dense forests, swamplands, savanna, and seacoast and has a corresponding wealth of animal and plant life. Benin is also home to many ethnic groups speaking a wide variety of languages. The land was once the seat of several native kingdoms, but it came under the rule of the French in the 19th century, during which time it was called Dahomey. It became an independent nation in 1960 and changed its named to Benin in 1975. French is still the national language, and the French influence in the culture remains strong. Nevertheless, native traditions, mixed with Western influences, are very much alive.

Historically, this part of Africa played an enormous role in the transatlantic slave trade. Indeed, the seaboard region of Benin came to be included in what was called the Slave Coast. During the 16th through the 19th centuries, around 10 million to 12 million African people were captured and sent to the Americas under brutal conditions to work as enslaved peoples. Conditions were so harsh and inhumane that 15 to 25 percent of the captives died aboard the ships. The departure point for millions of these ill-fated people was Ouidah, a town on the coast of Benin. Today, a memorial called the Door of No Return stands on a sandy beach there to commemorate the lives of those lost to one of the most terrible institutions in history.

The long-term repercussions of that human tragedy, followed by years of European colonialism, have left scars in Benin—and much of Africa—that are still visible today. Primarily, it is seen in the country's profound poverty, with the poor education and health systems that go along with it. Political instability has proven to be a common aftermath of colonial rule the world over, and Benin has had its fair share. Like a snake eating its own tail, the political turbulence that often follows joyous independence is both a cause and consequence of poverty. Benin suffered a particularly harsh period under the leadership of Mathieu Kerekou, who seized power in a military coup in 1972. He imposed single-party rule based on Marxist-Leninist ideology through 1990, a move that only deepened the country's impoverishment. Radicalism, inefficiency, and corruption undermined his regime, and he eventually changed course.

In the 1990s, the nation transitioned to a multiparty democracy. In fact, it earned a reputation as one of sub-Saharan Africa's most stable democracies. In 2019, however, that equilibrium was rocked by political events revolving around that year's electoral process. The nation's electoral commission blocked all opposition parties from participating in the election when it declared that only two political parties were eligible to run candidates for seats in the 83-member National Assembly. Both of those parties, as it just so happened, were loyal to President Patrice Talon, who had been in power since 2016. The move was supposedly made to try to impose some order on the excessive number of political parties in the nation—there were more than 200 of them in a country the size of Pennsylvania—but the extremely restrictive move triggered a backlash.

There were public protests and incidents of pre-election violence, including some deaths. Protests were banned, and protestors were arrested. Social media was blocked, and the internet nearly shut down entirely. Ultimately, only 23 percent of people voted in the 2019 election, a big drop from the 65 percent who had voted in the previous one.

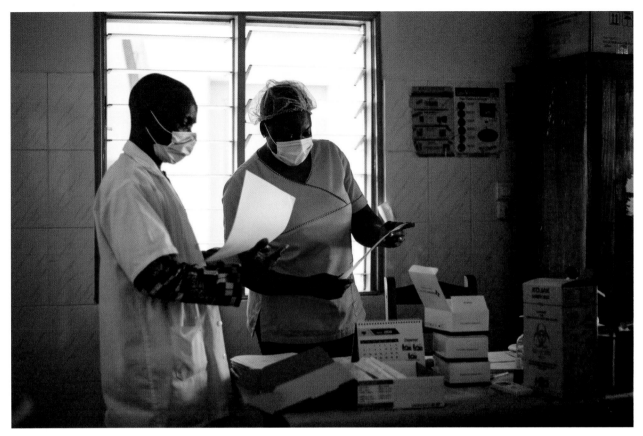

It was against that unsettled background that the COVID-19 pandemic hit the country in March 2020. The disease put a strain on an already weak health-care system. International agencies including the World Health Organization (WHO), the United Nations Children's Fund (UNICEF), and the International Federation of Red Cross and Red Crescent Societies (IFRC) jumped in to help the government address the crisis. Thirteen testing laboratories were established, and screening sites were set up at airports and the country's borders. Mobile screening sites traveled to institutions and businesses. People wore masks and remained home as much as possible, and travel to the country was severely restricted. The vigilance appeared to pay off. As of November 2020, Benin had recorded 2,844 cases of COVID-19, but only 43 deaths.

How the pandemic will end up affecting the economy and politics of this struggling nation remains to be seen.

Health workers prepare coronavirus tests at the Cadjehoun Health Center in Cotonou on May 9, 2020.

GEOGRAPHY

A flat, grassy landscape in Benin's plateau region extends to highlands in the far distance.

1

AFRICA IS AN ENORMOUS CONTINENT. In terms of area and population, it's the second-largest of Earth's seven continents, after Asia. However, Africa is composed of more countries than any other continent—it has 54 sovereign nations, and many of those are quite enormous as well. Algeria is the largest in area, while Nigeria has the most people. Some African countries, on the other hand, are tiny. The Gambia, on the continent's west coast, is the smallest of the mainland countries, while five island nations are even smaller.

Benin is one of Africa's smaller countries. With an area of 43,488 square miles (112,633 square kilometers), it's the 38th-largest nation on the continent. For comparison, Benin is slightly smaller than the state of Pennsylvania. It is narrow from east to west, with only a 75-mile (121-km) coastline in the south. From north to south, though, the country is about 430 miles (692 km) long. To the west, Benin borders Togo; to the east, Nigeria; and to the north, the countries Niger and Burkina Faso. To the south lies the Atlantic Ocean.

Benin is named for the body of water that forms its coastline on the Atlantic Ocean, the Bight of Benin. It's a bight, or bend, in the larger Gulf of Guinea, which forms the ocean's inner corner on the western side of the African continent.

Much of the south was once covered by rain forest, but most of this has been cleared during the centuries of human occupation. Some of the land was made into plantations where corn, cassava, palms, and cotton are grown. The rest is open savanna or is lightly forested.

LANDSCAPES

There are five main environmental zones within the country.

THE COAST   This is a low-lying, marshy region where the country's three main rivers empty into the Atlantic Ocean. Benin's coast also has several wide, sandy beaches with coconut palms. The landscape is dotted with lakes

Grand Popo, near the Benin/Togo border, has a long stretch of sandy beach but remains relatively undeveloped.

and lagoons. Coastal lagoons are shallow bodies of water connected to the sea through inlets; they are transitional zones between land and sea. The only access to the sea is through outlets from the Grand Popo and Cotonou lagoons. Benin has no natural harbor on the seacoast.

THE BARRE COUNTRY   This fertile clay area lies just north of the coast. It contains the Lama Marsh, a large swampy area. Here the landscape is generally flat, with occasional hills covered with palm groves.

THE PLATEAUS   These inland regions in the south are relatively flat areas at altitudes ranging between 66 and 656 feet (20 and 200 meters). They are covered by a mix of scrubby savannas, woodlands, and cropland. They are divided by river valleys running north to south. The four major plateaus are the Abomey, Ketou, Aplahoue, and Zagnanado.

This map of Benin shows surrounding countries and the Bight of Benin. It also shows Benin's capital city of Porto-Novo, other major cities, and main rivers.

THE ATAKORA MOUNTAINS   In the northwest region of Benin, the Atakora Department includes part of the Atakora Mountains, which extends to the west into neighboring Togo. (In fact, the range is also called the Togo Mountains.) These low mountains are the location of Benin's highest point, Mont Sokbaro, on the Togo border, which rises to a height of 2,159 ft (658 m).

THE NIGER DRAINAGE PLAINS   Much of Benin's northeast border with the country of Niger is formed by the Niger River, the main river of West Africa. Two of Benin's major rivers, the Alibouri and Sota, are tributaries of the Niger and branch off in this region. This part of Benin is also the location of W National Park (*Parc National du W*), which extends into Burkina Faso and Niger.

Since 1975, the United Nations Educational, Scientific and Cultural Organization (UNESCO) has maintained a list of international landmarks or regions considered to be of "outstanding value" to the people of the world. Such sites embody the common natural and cultural heritage of humanity and therefore deserve particular protection. The organization works with host countries to establish plans for managing and conserving their sites. UNESCO also reports on sites that are in imminent or potential danger of destruction and can offer emergency funds to try to save the property.

The organization is continually assessing new sites for inclusion on the World Heritage List. In order to be selected, a site must be of "outstanding universal value" and meet at least one of ten criteria. These required elements include cultural value—that is, artistic, religious, or historical significance—and natural value, including exceptional beauty, unusual natural phenomenon, and scientific importance.

As of November 2020, there are 1,121 sites listed: 869 cultural, 213 natural, and 39 mixed (cultural and natural) properties in 167 nations. Of those, 53 are listed as "in danger." Benin has two sites listed, one cultural and one natural. The cultural site is the Royal Palaces of Abomey, a group of 10 palaces from the Kingdom of Dahomey, spanning the period from 1625 to 1900. The other is the W-Arly-Pendjari Complex, an extension of the W National Park of Niger, which extends into Benin and Burkina Faso.

CLIMATE

In general, Benin has a tropical climate. It is hot and humid in the south and semiarid in the north, as the country stretches across two climatic zones. The north of the country experiences two seasons a year: a rainy season from May to September, when it receives between 37 and 48 inches (94 and 122 centimeters) of rain, and a dry season, when it can get as hot as 110 degrees Fahrenheit (43 degrees Celsius) in January. Between December and March, a dry wind, called the *harmattan*, blows from the desert north.

The southern part of the country experiences four seasons. The main rainy season runs from March to July. This is followed by a short, dry season that lasts through mid-September. A short rainy season then comes for two months, and between mid-November and March comes the main dry season.

Rainfall gets heavier the farther east in the country one travels, from 32 inches (81 cm) in Grand Popo to 50 inches (127 cm) in Porto-Novo. Temperatures rarely get above 95°F (35°C).

RIVERS AND LAGOONS

The Niger River constitutes the main drainage system of the country. The Niger is the third-longest river in Africa and arises in the highlands of Guinea. It passes through Mali, Niger, and Burkina Faso before crossing the border into Benin. The river drains around 1,380,000 square miles (3.57 million sq km) across West Africa.

Another major river is the Pendjari (also called the Oti), a tributary of the Volta River. It rises in Benin and flows for 240 miles (386 km), forming the border with Burkina Faso, before crossing into Togo.

Other rivers in Benin include the Mono, the Couffo, and the Oueme. These rivers arise in the central plains of Benin and form broad floodplains in the southern coastal zone.

A woman guides her small craft full of pineapples over Lake Nokoué in Ganvie, Benin.

Boats line the shore of Lake Nokoué (or Nokoué Lagoon) in this drone photograph.

The body of water to the south is part of the Atlantic Ocean. It is called the Bight of Benin. A bight is a wide, curving bay, and the word comes from the Old English *byht*, meaning a bend. This is the area that used to be called the Slave Coast.

Between the coast and the Atlantic lie the coastal lagoons. The main lagoons are in Cotonou, Ouidah, Grand Popo, and Porto-Novo. These lagoons are fed by the south-flowing rivers like the Oueme (or Weme) and are full of brackish water, which is a mix of river water and ocean water. The lagoons of Benin form just part of an extensive network of lagoons that stretches across West Africa's coast. The lagoons are separated by areas of dunes and sandbars. The complex flow of tides around the many obstructions makes navigating from the coast through the lagoons and into the open ocean extremely dangerous.

Lake Nokoué, or Nokoué Lagoon, the country's largest, covers 12,000 acres (4,856 hectares) and is, on average, only 5 feet (1.5 m) deep. It was permanently connected with the Atlantic Ocean during the latter half of the 20th century. Previous to this, the lake had been the site of a major fishery in Benin, supplying much of the fish sold in the market. Yields were especially high in the 1950s. Once the lagoon was permanently connected with the ocean, however, the

One of the most unusual towns in Benin is Ganvie, which is located on the northern end of Lake Nokoué—not on the lakeshore, but on the lake itself. This village is constructed of bamboo houses perched on stilts in the lagoon. The only way to get around in Ganvie is by pirogue (a type of canoe). Even the market of Ganvie is on the water, with women selling fish, fruits, and vegetables from their boats. Some people call Ganvie the African Venice. Approximately 20,000 people live there.

The village originated centuries ago during the era of the slave trade. The king of Dahomey was looking for more young men to sell to the Europeans in return for their goods. He especially wanted more guns in exchange. Some of the Tofinu people fled to swampy areas to escape enslavement and lived off the fish and other resources of the swamp around the lake. The swamp provided food and building materials as well as protection from the Dahomean king due to a religious restriction that kept him from sending his soldiers over the water. Finally, the Tofinu learned how to build

Shown here is an aerial view of the lake city of Ganvie.

their houses and live right on the lake surface itself. The name of their village breaks down to gan ("we are saved"), and vie ("community").

The village is a popular tourist destination in Benin and is on UNESCO's World Heritage Tentative List, which means it's being considered as a World Heritage site.

rise in the salt level of the water (salinity) seriously hurt the fishing industry in this area.

To combat the problem of falling fish stocks, some fishermen in Benin have turned to acadja fisheries to help them farm fish. In acadja fisheries, branches are placed upright in the water, forming a kind of corral for the fish. The preferred material for the branches is bamboo, as it lasts longer and because algae, which some species of fish eat readily, grow on the surface of the bamboo. This means the fishermen do not have to feed the fish. Because of acadja enclosures, the populations of some species of fish in the lagoon are stabilizing or increasing. The most successful is a species of native tilapia called the blackchin, or *Sarotherodon melanotheron*, which can tolerate higher salinity than other freshwater fish of the area.

Benin is a country that crosses several environmental and climatic zones, from the river valley of the Niger to the tropical lagoons of the coast. The range of climates supports a wide variety of plants, animals, and crops, including fish farms. Benin's wealth of water has helped its people farm much of the country and even supports those who make their homes on lakes.

Red Star Square marks the major urban center of Cotonou.

CITIES

Most of the nation's people live in the southern part of the country. Benin's two largest cities are Porto-Novo, the official capital, and Cotonou, the de facto capital. Both are located near the coast. Porto-Novo is a port on an inlet, and its name comes from the Portuguese for "New Port;" it was originally built in the 1600s as a port for the Portuguese slave trade. In 2018, the city had an estimated population of about 285,000.

Although Porto-Novo is the constitutional capital, the main government buildings are located in Cotonou, which is Benin's largest city. In 2017, that city's population was reportedly 692,000. Both cities are in the delta of the Oueme River, Benin's largest river, which flows into the Atlantic between them. Like Porto-Novo, Cotonou was founded as a port for the slave trade—but later, in 1830. Today, it is the location of the country's only international airport.

INTERNET LINKS

eros.usgs.gov/westafrica/country/republic-benin
This US Geological Survey site includes images of the geographical landscapes in Benin.

whc.unesco.org/en/statesparties/bj
This is the World Heritage page for Benin.

www.worldatlas.com/articles/ganvie-benin-unique-places-around-the-world.html
This site takes a quick look at the village of Ganvie.

HISTORY

This funerary crown from the Kingdom of Dahomey dates from 1860 to 1889. The artifact, part of an extensive African arts collection at the Musée du quai Branly—Jacques Chirac in Paris, France, is one of the national treasures that Benin has requested be returned.

2

BEFORE THE MODERN STATE NOW known as Benin was established, it was home to a number of overlapping cultures and kingdoms. Various ethnic peoples lived in the region over many millennia, but little is known about ancient times.

The history of West Africa has been shaped by many forces, one of which has been the continued spread of the Sahara Desert since the end of the last ice age. As the desert moved south, displaced people moved ahead of it in repeated waves of migration. These people brought new farming and metalworking techniques, as well as new ideas, to the area that would one day be Benin. Because these people did not appear to have brought new languages, it would seem they arrived in small groups and adopted the languages of the people around them.

Over the centuries, people became more proficient with using metal and with farming. By 1400 CE, they were forming the first of what would later become great city-states. At this point, the realm of archaeology combines with oral tradition—and a bit later, with written history— to record the kings and kingdoms that dominated Benin from this time onward.

DAHOMEY

Part of Benin was once home to the Kingdom of Dahomey. The oral traditions of the area tell of a people called the Adja, who migrated into the area that is now Benin during the 12th or 13th century.

The history of the nation of Benin should not be confused with that of the Kingdom of Benin. Although several kingdoms ruled in regions of today's Benin, the Kingdom of Benin, or the Benin Empire, was not one of them. That historic kingdom existed in what is now southern Nigeria.

People are shown here arriving at the 2018 funeral of Dah Dedjalagni Agoli-Agbo, a king of the ancestral throne of Dahomey. Modern-day kings have no formal powers in Benin but retain ceremonial and political influence.

The Adja founded a village called Allada. Within a few centuries, this small village had grown into the center of a large state called Allada (also called Ardra), which was ruled by kings assisted by respected elders. Around the year 1620, three brothers had a disagreement over which one of them would be king of Allada. One took the throne of Allada, one founded the city that is now Porto-Novo, and one founded the kingdom of Abomey. Abomey later became the center of the Kingdom of Dahomey on the Abomey Plateau.

Each successor of the first king of Dahomey pledged to leave his own successor with a bigger kingdom than he had inherited. Thus, they were largely concerned with wars of expansion, fueling a slave trade that made the kingdom very wealthy. Many of the war captives were sold to the Europeans as enslaved peoples. The kingdom was a major trading partner of Europeans, selling cloth, ivory, and enslaved Africans to Dutch, French, and Portuguese traders.

Portuguese sailors first explored the coastal region of Benin in 1472—about two decades before Christopher Columbus would sail to the Americas. The African peoples' first contact with the Europeans didn't turn into much until about 1553, when real trade began. Among the principal "goods" traded were captive peoples who were sold to European merchants to be enslaved. Most of these enslaved people were shipped over the Atlantic to the Americas, where they were forced to work in the territories that Europeans had seized there. As sugar, tobacco, and cotton plantations were developed in the Americas, the need for forced human labor increased sharply, and the trade flourished for several centuries. Many enslaved people were taken from the area of modern Benin, and the resulting depopulation and cultural ramifications have had a long-lasting destructive effect.

A carved tree trunk in the center of Ouidah commemorates the region's role in the slave trade.

The development of the transatlantic slave trade altered both African and American history forever.

Dahomey was a despotic and militaristic kingdom, well situated for defense. It was founded on a plateau that had more open vegetation than the tropical rain forests of the south, and it was bounded by rivers on the east and west. To the north rose steep hills, and to the south was a swamp. Approaching the capital of Abomey unseen would be very difficult, and taking the kingdom by surprise with a large army would be impossible.

On the plateau itself, rainfall was generous, with the area receiving an average of 43 inches (109 cm) of rain per year. This allowed the people to grow a wide variety of crops, including millet, corn, cassava, beans, cotton, and oil palms. Thus the kings of Dahomey had a well-fed population who could contribute materials and people toward any war effort.

WOMEN IN DAHOMEY

One of the unique features of the Dahomean kingdom was a dependence upon women to perform many court functions, even taking on military roles. The king was the only man permitted to live in the palace, so any court functions that took place within the palace were performed by him or by women.

A very important function was that of reign-mate, or *kpojito*. This woman never came from within the royal family but was instead a commoner. Choosing a commoner as kpojito may have been to symbolize the union of the king with the people of his kingdom.

The kpojito did not help run the kingdom, but she did perform many important ritual functions. She had her own household and retinue and was forbidden to have any contact with men other than the king. Because of this, she was a shadowy figure to the Europeans who had contacts with Dahomey, and they left no records relating the full scope of the kpojito's duties. However, it is known that during the 19th century, the kpojito heard legal cases having to do with religious crimes and made judgments that could be appealed only to the king himself.

Another woman with influence in court was the *daklo*. She was the intermediary between the king and the people who came to petition him or came at his summons. No one, not even a person who had been summoned,

Perhaps the most interesting way in which women served the king of Dahomey was as soldiers in the army. These female warrior corps existed from about 1645 until 1905. The female soldiers of Dahomey, called the Mino (and sometimes referred to as the Dahomey Amazons), were raised from an early age to fight hand to hand and with various kinds of weapons. They were trained to be strong and to

The Mino are pictured in this photograph dating from about 1890.

endure suffering. Their tutors also instructed them on hunting, dancing, and playing musical instruments. Still, even though they might have some skill with music or dance, the women were not inclined toward romance or a soft life. They lived only for war. When sent into battle, they rushed into it headlong, screaming their battle cries, and fought furiously. Those who described them said they appeared to be immune to fear and pain. Neighbors of Dahomey lived in terror of them.

The women warriors of Dahomey were foot soldiers. The women's main weapons were muskets, machetes, and clubs, and for the most part they did not use shields. The battle dress for the women was a half-sleeved rust-colored tunic. It was tucked in at the waist by a belt. The women also wore shorts that fell to the knees, and they fought barefoot. Around their foreheads they tied white headbands.

could see the king directly. Instead the person lay on the ground on one side of a palm-leaf barrier and pled his case to the daklo on the other side. The daklo went to the king with his words and then returned to the petitioner with the king's response. Powerful men often tried to influence the daklo, since only she could relate their words to the king, and they wanted to make sure she would relay their words in the most flattering and positive way possible.

Royal women performed services for the king as well, including dispensing his justice. If the king wished to discipline someone, he would send out a large party of his wives to destroy or confiscate that person's property. Since touching a royal woman was a crime punishable by death, the person being disciplined could do nothing but stand aside and watch the women take or ruin his possessions.

Another function the royal women served was as spies for the king. Traditionally all women married into their husband's family in Dahomey, and their children belonged to the father, with the exception of princesses. Royal women married, but neither they nor their children were part of the husband's family. Instead, their loyalty was always to the king, and they would report back to the palace concerning the activities in their husbands' households. By marrying princesses to powerful men, the king had access to detailed information about these men, down to what happened in their own homes.

THE END OF THE KINGDOM

The kingdom of Dahomey expanded rapidly. In 1724, it captured the neighboring kingdom of Allada, and in 1727, it captured another kingdom, Ouidah. Capturing Ouidah, a coastal city, gave Dahomey access to the sea. This also gave Dahomey access to trade with the Europeans, especially the French, who had built a fort there in 1704. However, the Yoruba kingdom of Oyo, which was situated to the east of Dahomey, was strong enough to conquer Dahomey in 1730. It was not until 1818, under King Ghézo, that Dahomey regained its independence.

During the 1800s, the kingdom was at its largest and most powerful, but by 1900, the French had deposed the last Dahomean king. A series of two Franco-Dahomean wars took place in the early 1890s, with the French emerging victorious. The Fon people of Dahomey were accustomed to hand-to-hand combat with swords and machetes, but they proved no match for the French bayonets. Dahomey then came under French rule.

THE SCRAMBLE FOR AFRICA

The nations of Africa are a relatively modern creation. As recently as the 19th century, vast regions of the continent's interior remained unmapped and unknown to the outside world. Native peoples lived in various tribal kingdoms with their own rich cultures and traditions. To Europe and the rest of the Western world, though, Africa was "the dark continent"—unexplored and largely unknown.

Africa's seacoast regions were more accessible and therefore better known to Europeans. Beginning in the 14th century, Portugal and other nations set up trading posts, forts, and attempted colonies along coastal areas. The transatlantic slave trade, dominated by the Portuguese, and later the Dutch, the French, and the British, operated out of the West African coastal region—and the area around the Bight of Benin became known as the Slave Coast. It was a departure point for captured people who were then shipped across the Atlantic to the Americas.

In terms of colonization, however, European powers were at first more interested in the Americas. North Africa had long been dominated by Muslim cultures and was essentially a barrier to Europe. However, the European colonies in the Americas eventually won their independence. At the same time, the Industrial Revolution was radically changing Western economies and ways of life. For a variety of reasons, Europe took another look at Africa.

Ongoing piracy along the Barbary Coast and a trade dispute between France and Algiers in North Africa sparked the French invasion of Algiers in 1830. By 1875, the French conquest was complete. Meanwhile, European leaders sent explorers into the heart of Africa to map it, convinced that the African people needed the "civilizing" influence of European culture.

Europe therefore began to see Africa as ripe for the taking, and a virtual land grab began. By 1884–1885, what has come to be called "the Scramble for Africa" was on. A new age of imperialism began in which major Western powers tried to secure and gain supremacy by building an empire of overseas properties. Colonies were a status symbol as well as a source of native resources, labor, and military recruits.

In 1884, 13 European countries met in Berlin to draw up the rules of African colonization and literally split the continent among themselves. The colonizing powers were primarily Britain and France, with Germany, Italy, Portugal, Belgium, and Spain taking the rest. Lines of new nations were drawn arbitrarily, sometimes cutting apart historically tribal regions. By 1902, 90 percent of Africa was under European control. By 1914, the European takeover of Africa was complete, with only Ethiopia managing to remain sovereign.

FRENCH RULE

After the French had moved into the area and effectively conquered the local kingdoms, they began their colonial rule. Missionaries established missions, and schools were set up. Most of these activities took place in the south of the country, with fewer missionaries and educators being found the farther one got from the coast. The French also tried to increase the agricultural potential of the country. Mineral resources were few and located inland, which made them hard to exploit.

French Dahomey was a French colony from 1894 to 1958. It became an overseas territory of France in 1946 and became self-governing as a part of the French Community in 1958.

INDEPENDENCE AND INSTABILITY

Dahomey, as it was known, won its independence from France on August 1, 1960. At that time, the country had a weak economy and a population splintered into many ethnic and regional divisions. Factions within the major political party of the time, the Dahomeyean Progressive Union, kept the nation destabilized with conflicts and power plays among members.

Within a short time, three main political groups emerged under strong leaders. One was in the southeast under Sourou-Migan Apithy, a leader from the Yoruba. Another, in the Fon and Adja areas in the center and southwest of the country, was led by Justin Ahomadegbe, a descendent of a royal family. The third was in the north under Hubert Maga, a former school teacher turned politician who could count on the Bariba vote. When Dahomey gained its independence from France in 1960, Maga was appointed to the presidency and was officially elected to that post on December 11.

Shown here are French language newspapers from January 1947, published in the countries of French West Africa (AOF). The AOF was a federation created in 1895 of eight French colonial territories in Africa: Mauritania, Senegal, Niger, French Sudan (now Mali), French Guinea (now Guinea), Ivory Coast, Upper Volta (now Burkina Faso), and Dahomey (now Benin).

The 1960s in Dahomey were a time of political infighting, student strikes, and strikes by trade unions. The first major collapse occurred on October 28, 1963. The government had been championing austerity policies designed to make the country more fiscally stable. At the same time, however, many government officials were corrupt and spent large amounts of money on luxuries. This led to massive demonstrations.

President Maga was deposed in a coup led by the army's chief of staff, Colonel Christophe Soglo, and in 1964, Sourou-Migan Apithy was elected president. He didn't last long, however, and was forced out in 1965. Another new government was created with Tahirou Congacou, president of the National Assembly, in charge. However, Congacou was not able to work with others well enough to form a stable government, and three months later, Soglo himself assumed control of the country.

Colonel Christophe Soglo addresses a crowd in Cotonou after leading a military coup on October 28, 1963.

In 1967, a group of junior army officers ousted Soglo and replaced him with Major Maurice Kouandete. According to popular belief, Soglo learned he had been ousted when someone knocked on his door and said, "You're through." Indeed, no regime leader was killed during any of Dahomey's numerous coups during this time.

Kouandete, like his predecessors, could not get political rivals to stop fighting long enough to form a stable government, and his administration also failed quickly.

A presidential election was to be held in 1968 in an attempt to resolve the situation, but old leaders such as Apithy called for a boycott of the election, and 83 percent of the electorate stayed home. In the wake of this disaster, another military regime was formed under physician Emile-Derlin Zinsou, but it lasted only until December 10, 1969. Zinsou was soon removed from power by Kouandete, but the officer corps of the army refused to recognize him as the leader of the country.

Instead, the army proposed a military directorate that would be led by several men; however, these men also could not put aside their differences. Elections were held, with the situation after the elections resembling the situation of a decade before, with Apithy, Ahomadegbe, and Maga winning the vote in the southeast, the southwest and central, and the north, respectively.

The directorate suspended the results of the elections, and in consequence, each section of Dahomey threatened to secede from the others. Finally Maga, Apithy, and Ahomadegbe agreed to serve as "co-presidents." Maga was the first of the triumvirate to serve as president with a two-year term. In 1972, Ahomadegbe assumed the presidency for what was supposed to be the next two years. Their terms were marked, like those of their predecessors, by fiscal mismanagement and corruption.

PEOPLE'S REPUBLIC OF BENIN (1975-1990)

On October 26, 1972, the army launched its sixth coup d'état. Although at the time it did not seem much different from the other five, this one would change the country forever. This particular coup was orchestrated by officers from the Ouidah garrison, who recruited Major Mathieu Kerekou to lead the new regime. Anyone connected to the former government was retired or placed under arrest in military camps away from their bases of power.

During the 1970s, Kerekou moved the country toward a Marxist-Leninist Communist government, one in which the state was in control of nearly every business and economic activity. Consequently, foreign investment in the country—never very sizeable to begin with—dried up. In 1975, the country of Dahomey was renamed the People's Republic of Benin. The army and the political system were reorganized to reflect the new political climate. A new constitution endorsed the new political organization and decreed a joining of civil and military authority positions.

The People's Revolutionary Party became the only political party. However, the revolutionary government failed to live up to its ideology. What little natural resources the country had were squandered, and the economy was in turmoil.

Some areas did see progress, as roads and tourist facilities reached into the northern half of the country where they never had before. Cotton production, too, began to rise. However, Benin's problems were too large to be offset much by these small gains.

Reorganization of the educational system resulted in a mass exodus of trained teachers from the country. Other professionals also left the country in great numbers. As a result, despite a high birth rate, the overall population of the country did not increase. The lack of trained people in a number of professions severely hampered industry and education.

The difficulty the ruling military regime had in controlling the country spilled over into the regime itself. Cabinet meetings erupted into fistfights. Ministers argued with each other endlessly. Key areas of government were practically frozen, unable to perform their functions.

By 1981, around 92 percent of the country's budget had been designated as payroll for bureaucrats. The need for income resulted in Benin signing an agreement with France to take its nuclear waste for only 10 percent of what other nations charged. Money from offshore oil wells helped, but it was not enough. In 1989, mass demonstrations against the government spurred a governmental collapse. Riots broke out, and there was no money to pay or supply the army. The banking system collapsed. The nuclear-waste contracts were canceled after it came to light that Kerekou planned to bury the waste near Abomey, a move the southerners felt was designed by a northern ruler to eliminate them.

DEMOCRACY

Kerekou had to accept that his Marxist revolution had failed and the country was in desperate straits. His own aide, the Archbishop of Cotonou, and France urged Kerekou to assemble a national convention to discuss how to solve the nation's problems. He did, and a nine-day convention was held. Even ex-regime leaders and Beninese living abroad attended. Kerekou's 18-year reign was criticized by everyone, and Kerekou, with no way to pay for continued military rule, was forced to accept the convention's advice. A new constitution was drawn up and ratified on December 10, 1990. Political prisoners were

Patrice Talon, president of the Republic of Benin, welcomes guests to the presidential palace in Cotonou for the Independence Day celebrations on August 1, 2020.

released, and Marxism was abandoned. Benin would become a democracy, and multiparty elections would be held in 1991.

By the time of the elections, 34 political parties had been organized, and 1,400 people were running for 65 seats in the National Assembly. Fourteen men ran for president, but the only serious contenders for the job were Nicephore Soglo (a cousin of Christophe Soglo) and Kerekou. Each won his own area of the country: Soglo the south and Kerekou the north. Soglo was elected president, and his party won most of the seats in the National Assembly.

Kerekou ran successfully for the presidency in 1996, ousting Soglo, who won the seat of mayor of Cotonou in February 2002. In 2006, Thomas Boni Yayi (or Yayi Boni) won the presidential election, defeating Adrien Houngbédji with 75 percent of the vote. He was re-elected in 2011 and served until 2016.

Throughout these years, several of the presidents (Soglo and Boni Yayi in particular) tried to institute economic reform, and Benin was seen as one of Africa's most stable democracies. However, political problems and corruption continued. In 2012, during Boni Yayi's term, an alleged plot to poison the president was uncovered, with the mastermind being his former ally, the wealthy businessman Patrice Talon. At that point, Talon fled to France after being accused of embezzling more than $20 million in taxes. Boni Yayi eventually pardoned Talon in 2014, a move he would probably come to regret.

THE TALON YEARS

Talon ran for president in 2016, and after a runoff against then-Prime Minister Lionel Zinsou, he won the office. At the time, Talon was listed as the 15th richest person in sub-Saharan Africa, worth around $400 million. He had become wealthy in Benin's cotton trade in the 1980s and was often called the "King of Cotton."

As president, Talon instituted changes that caused concern in the international community. His tenure brought crackdowns on free speech and a restriction of civil liberties. Talon effectively excluded all opposition parties from participating in the parliamentary elections of April 2019. People took to the streets in protest, and the police fired on the crowds; at least two people were killed. Security forces surrounded the home of former president Boni Yayi, a leader of the opposition, who was held essentially under house arrest. The following June, he abruptly left the country for supposed health reasons. He returned the following November but was unable to meet with Talon.

Meanwhile, as of late 2020, international observers fear a shift to authoritarianism under Talon and are watching the situation in Benin with dismay.

INTERNET LINKS

www.bbc.com/news/world-africa-13040372
This timeline of key events in the history of Benin begins in 1946.

www.britannica.com/place/Benin
The online encyclopedia provides a reliable account of Benin's history.

www.nytimes.com/2019/07/04/world/africa/benin-protests-talon-yayi.html
This article looks at the developments in Benin under the rule of Patrice Talon.

GOVERNMENT

Patrice Talon (*left*) receives a national flag during his swearing in as the president of Benin in the capital Porto-Novo.

3

THE REPUBLIC OF BENIN IS A presidential democratic republic. That means the nation is led by a president as the chief executive, with separate legislative and judicial branches. Theoretically, if not always in practice, people elect representatives to the government in free and fair elections, and multiple political parties exist to represent the various political views of the people. Suffrage is universal, beginning at age 18.

The capital of Benin is Porto-Novo, but the seat of government, where most of the country's government buildings are located and most governmental activity takes place, is Cotonou. Benin is a secular nation, meaning the government operates separately from any particular religious group. There is no official national religion.

Like many other nations with a recent colonial history, however, Benin has only existed as an independent nation for a few decades, and it is still struggling to find its footing. From 1975 to 1990, it was run as a Marxist-Socialist state, which proved to be a debacle. At that point, it shifted to a democratic form of government, and since then, Benin has been heralded as one of Africa's most stable and successful democracies.

Whether it is still operating as such is another question. In 2019, with Benin under the leadership of President Patrice Talon, the Democracy Index rated it a "hybrid regime." The index is compiled every two years

The flag of Benin is divided into three color fields–green, yellow, and red. A vertical band on the hoist side is green, and two equal horizontal bands are yellow (*top*) and red (*bottom*). The green symbolizes hope and revival, the yellow represents the wealth of the nation, and the red is for the courage of the people and their ancestors.

by the Economist Intelligence Unit, a research and analysis company in the United Kingdom. The index measures the state of democracies in the world's nations, categorizing them as one of four regime types: full democracies, flawed democracies, hybrid regimes, and authoritarian regimes. Hybrid regimes are defined as "nations with regular electoral frauds, preventing them from being fair and free democracies. These nations commonly have governments that apply pressure on political opposition, non-independent judiciaries, widespread corruption, harassment and pressure placed on the media, anemic rule of law, and more pronounced faults than flawed democracies in the realms of underdeveloped political culture, low levels of participation in politics, and issues in the functioning of governance."

THE CONSTITUTION

The most recent version of the nation's constitution dates to 1990. The constitution affirms the sovereignty of the nation, expresses its values and its commitment to peace, establishes the rights and responsibilities of the people, and spells out the structure and powers of the three branches of government. The preamble, or introduction, to the constitution admits to the nation's "turbulent constitutional and political evolution since its accession to independence." However, it asserts that "the successive changes of political regimes and of governments have not blunted the determination of the Beninese people to search for, in their own spirit, the cultural, philosophical and spiritual values of civilization which sustain the forms of their patriotism."

The constitution grants the Beninese people various rights and freedoms. These include the right to life, liberty, and security; the freedom of religion; freedom of expression; and freedom of the press. It guarantees equality of all people before the law, including the equality of men and women. It also recognizes the right to work and the right to strike.

In practice, however, certain constitutional guarantees are not always enforced. For example, although Article 24 ensures freedom of the press, the nation's commitment to journalistic freedom appears to be slipping. The 2020 World Press Freedom Index compiled by Reporters Without Borders ranked Benin at number 113, and trending downward, out of 180 nations. The

U.S. Department of State's 2018 Report on Human Rights Practices in Benin documents a number of governmental abuses of several constitutional rights, freedoms, and protections.

Other international organizations, however, such as the World Bank, have not been so quick to conclude Benin is drifting away from democracy. The World Bank has stated, "Benin is a stable democracy, despite some tension surrounding the legislative elections held on April 28, 2019."

Women take part in a peaceful protest march in Cotonou on March 11, 2019. The demonstration was organized by opposition political parties to denounce their exclusion from the coming election process.

THE EXECUTIVE

The president is both the head of government and the head of state. He (or she, but as of 2020 there has not been a female president) is elected by the people to a five-year term. They may serve a maximum of two terms, either in succession

or apart. As of late 2020, the president is Patrice Talon, who was elected in 2016 and is eligible for another term. The next election is scheduled for 2021. The president is responsible for guaranteeing national independence, territorial integrity, and respect for the constitution, treaties, and other international agreements.

To be eligible to run for presidency, a person must be Beninese by birth or have been a citizen for at least 10 years. The candidate must be at least 40 but no more than 70 years old, must live in Benin, and must be considered healthy, both physically and mentally, by a committee of three doctors appointed by a constitutional court.

The president appoints the cabinet, the Council of Ministers. These people advise the president and manage the day-to-day departmental operations of their particular areas of expertise, in accordance with the president's programs and policies.

Benin's president Patrice Talon (*left*) meets United Nations (UN) Secretary-General Antonio Guterres at the UN headquarters in New York City.

THE LEGISLATURE

Benin has a unicameral, or one-house, legislative body, the National Assembly. It consists of 83 members who are elected by direct popular vote to four-year terms. Members are called MPs (members of parliament), with constituencies corresponding to Benin's 12 departments, which are like states or provinces.

The National Assembly meets for two sessions each year. The first session starts in the first half of April, and the second begins in the first half of October. These sessions cannot last any longer than three months. If the president wishes, they can call an emergency session during those times of the year when the National Assembly is not already meeting. These emergency sessions cannot be any longer than 15 days.

Benin's National Assembly meets in Porto-Novo on May 16, 2019.

THE COURTS

The judicial system of Benin consists of a Supreme Court, a Constitutional Court, and a High Court of Justice. The laws of Benin generally follow French civil law, though some "traditional" laws are also recognized.

The Supreme Court is the highest court. It consists of the chief justice and "not more than 20" justices (as of 2020 there are 16), organized into an administrative division, judicial chamber, and chamber of accounts. Members are appointed by the president after being recommended by the National Judicial Council and confirmed by the National Assembly. They must retire at age 70. Once the Supreme Court has made a decision in a case, there can be no appeals. The court is responsible for restraining the president and the National

Assembly from abusing their powers; for overseeing decisions rendered by lower courts; for controlling the accounts of the election campaigns; and for providing advice on the legality of bills before they can become laws.

The Constitutional Court of Benin is composed of seven people. The National Assembly appoints four of these judges, and the president of the republic appoints the other three. Members are appointed for five-year terms, which can be renewed.

A woman arrives to vote at an elementary school in Cotonou on Benin's election day in 2019.

The High Court of Justice exists exclusively to hear cases of high treason by either the sitting president or other members of the government while in office.

LOCAL GOVERNMENT

The French had originally divided what is now Benin into six départements, which were administrative units similar to the states in the United States. The six départements were Atakora, Atlantique, Borgou, Mono, Oueme, and Zou. These were subdivided into 35 sous-préfectures and further subdivided into 75 arrondissements.

In 1974, the départements were renamed provinces, and the sous-préfectures were renamed districts. The six provinces retained their old boundaries but were subdivided into 84 districts and subdivided again into 404 communes. Advisory councils were set up at the district and province levels. These councils were given the power to make decisions on local matters, policymaking, and finance. However, this organizational structure broke down and was gone by the mid-1990s.

On January 15, 1999, the country's six provinces were divided into 12 departments: Alibori, Atakora, Atlantique, Borgou, Collines, Donga, Kouffo, Littoral, Mono, Oueme, Plateau, and Zou. In 2008, each department was assigned an administrative capital. The departments in the north are larger in area, and those near the coast are smaller, as the population density there is greater.

INTERNET LINKS

www.cia.gov/library/publications/resources/the-world-factbook/geos/bn.html
This site provides up-to-date information about Benin's government.

www.constituteproject.org/constitution/Benin_1990.pdf?lang=en
An English-language version of the constitution of Benin is provided as a pdf.

www.gouv.bj
This is the website of the government of the Republic of Benin, which can be translated online into English.

rsf.org/en/benin
The Reporters Without Borders assessment of Benin's press freedom is provided here.

www.state.gov/reports/2018-country-reports-on-human-rights-practices/benin
This is the 2018 U.S. Department of State report on human rights practices in Benin.

ECONOMY

The West African CFA franc, the currency of Benin and several other African nations, was due to be replaced by a common currency called the eco in 2020, but the switch was delayed.

B ENIN'S ECONOMY HAS BEEN growing. After a disastrous experiment with Marxist-Leninist Communism in the 1970s and 1980s, Benin's change to a free-market system in 1990 helped the country regain some stability and growth in its economy. Recent years have seen impressive economic growth, but the country still struggles to improve its infrastructure, reduce poverty, create a more diverse economy, attract foreign investment, and broaden its foreign markets.

When President Patrice Talon took office in April 2016, he implemented a challenging plan to boost development throughout the country. One of the major obstacles to economic growth in Benin has been the nation's very incomplete infrastructure, particularly its electrical grid—the complex network that produces power and delivers it to consumers. Many areas of Benin were off the grid, meaning they had no electrical power at all, and those that did have electricity often found it to be spotty. Without universal, reliable electricity, Benin's economic growth has been hindered.

In recent years, access to electricity has improved, and blackouts have been considerably reduced. However, the process is far from complete.

4

Benin is one of 15 countries that make up the Economic Community of West African States (ECOWAS). Formed in 1975, this political and economic union strives for "collective self-sufficiency" by creating a single trade bloc. It also serves as a force for political stability with its own justice, financial, health, and anti-terrorism institutions, and it forms a coalition of peacekeeping military forces in times of political unrest in its member states.

WHAT IS GDP?

Gross domestic product (GDP) is a measure of a country's total production. The number reflects the total value of goods and services produced over one year. Economists use it to determine whether a country's economy is growing or contracting. Growth is good, while a falling GDP means trouble. Dividing the GDP by the number of people in the country determines the GDP per capita (per person). This number provides an indication of a country's average standard of living—the higher the better.

In 2017, the GDP per capita (adjusted to purchasing power parity) in Benin was approximately $2,300. That figure is considered quite low, and it ranked Benin at 201st out of 229 countries listed by the CIA World Factbook. *For comparison, the United States that year was number 19, with a GDP per capita of $59,500; France was number 40 with $44,000. Among the nations of mainland West Africa, Benin's neighbor Nigeria (number 165) had the highest GDP per capita that year at $5,900, while Niger (number 224), its neighbor to the north, had the lowest, with $1,200.*

Meanwhile, private, foreign direct investment, which is critical to emerging economies like Benin's, remains small, although a large proportion of the nation's infrastructure projects have been funded by foreign aid.

AGRICULTURE

From 2017 to 2019, agriculture contributed about 26.1 percent to Benin's GDP and employed about 38.6 percent of its labor force.

Until the 1970s, much of what was exported from the country came from the palm plantations. However, the profits from palm products had never been enough to fuel a great deal of economic growth, employment opportunities, and social services. After the 1970s, exports of cotton and the production of oil from offshore oil fields increased the country's wealth. The oil fields have since ceased production, but agriculture remains an important sector of Benin's economy.

The "king of crops" is cotton; it accounts for around 80 percent of the country's exports. In 2019, Benin was the leading cotton producer in

West Africa, followed by Mali and Burkina Faso. Benin's cotton yield in 2019 was significantly higher than it was when Talon first assumed office. The increase is attributed to the government's investment, in collaboration with private businesses, in modernizing the entire cotton supply chain. Not incidentally, Talon himself earned his personal fortune in the cotton business.

However, Benin's economy is easily affected by the world market prices for cotton, which rise and fall. The country, therefore, cannot afford to rely too heavily on just one crop. Cashews, shea nuts and shea butter, pineapples, palm products, and some cocoa and coffee also are export crops.

Most of the country's agriculture, however, is subsistence farming. Farmers grow food for themselves and their families, and survival is the economic

Farmers stand beside piles of white cotton bolls in the village of Naouari in central Benin.

In August 2019, Nigeria closed its 503-mile (809 km) border with Benin without warning. The reason was the high level of smuggling that was going on. The smuggling of goods across national borders has a long history between the two countries, particularly the smuggling of gasoline and rice.

Beninese smugglers cross into Nigeria, load up on gasoline there, and sneak it back into Benin, where they can sell it for more money. Nigeria is an oil-producing country, and the federal government subsidizes the price of fuel for its people. Therefore, gasoline bought in Nigeria costs only about half what customers in Benin and other West African countries pay. Many Beninese people will gladly pay a lower price, even though the smuggled fuel is often watered down and therefore of lower quality. In Benin, smuggled gas is known as kpayo *and is sold at roadside stands by people who have often been in the smuggling trade for many years. The Beninese authorities are usually willing to look the other way.*

The smuggling of rice works in the opposite direction. Nigeria has a restrictive trade policy and imposes high tariffs (additional fees) or even import bans on many products. The Nigerian government does this to encourage local production and economic self-sufficiency. The result, however, is that imports—such as rice—from other countries are much less expensive in Benin and other neighboring markets than they are in Nigeria. Rice and other goods are smuggled into Nigeria, where they can be sold for a profit while still selling below Nigeria's market price.

driver. They rarely produce enough of a surplus to sell or trade beyond what is necessary to buy the things they cannot grow themselves, such as tools and clothing. Subsistence farmers typically rely on traditional methods, as they have little money to invest in new equipment and processes. As a result, their yields tend to be low.

Small-scale farmers mostly grow grains, such as corn (maize), sorghum, and millet. Other important crops include cassava, yams, rice, tomatoes, peanuts, oranges, pineapples, and coconuts. Many farms are no larger than 2.5 acres (1 ha).

Ships unload cargo
at the port
of Cotonou.

INDUSTRY

Benin has very little industry, though in the future, with more reliable access to energy and transportation, industries are likely to move into the country and be successful. Textiles (mostly cotton), food processing, and construction materials and cement are the main industries.

The country has cement plants in Onigbolo and Pobe. There are palm-oil processing plants in Ahozon, Avrankou, Bohicon, Cotonou, Gbada, and Pobe, and there is a sugar refinery in Save. The West African Development Bank assisted in revitalizing a textile factory in Parakou. Other industries include two shrimp-processing plants, a soft-drink plant, a brewery, and several cotton-ginning facilities.

MINERALS

Benin has several exploitable natural resources, including gold, iron ore, phosphates, and petroleum.

Gold is found in the Atakora Mountains in the northwestern part of the country, along the Perma River. Mining began during the colonial era; the government of Benin itself took up gold mining in the mid-1960s. However, the effort was abandoned in the mid-1980s. After that, individuals from northern Benin, joined by migrant miners from the countries of Burkina Faso and Togo, began to mine for gold in the area.

The land is still held by the government of Benin, and in 1996, the government used militia to confiscate the mining equipment and personal property of the miners in an effort to halt their unregulated activities. The miners refused to be run off, and eventually the government accepted their presence and officially began to allow small-scale mining.

In 1982, Benin began producing petroleum from two wells from the Seme oil field. Average production began around 8,000 barrels a day, but this amount dwindled over time to approximately 1,900 barrels a day. In 1998, the oil field was shut down, but pumping resumed in 2013.

Deposits of phosphates have been identified in both northern and southern areas of the country. So far, exploitation of these resources has been determined to be uneconomical, and they remain undeveloped.

One of the reasons that such resources remain undeveloped is that they are in remote, inaccessible areas. Recent improvements in infrastructure, such as the Djougou-N'dali national road project, which connects Benin with Nigeria and Togo, may eventually change this.

ELECTRICITY AND FUEL

Few people in Benin have access to reliable electricity, and the demand for it rises every year. In the north of the country, especially, people are used to frequent disruptions in their service. These brownouts not only interrupt people's lives, but also slow economic development. In 2019, approximately 33 percent of Benin's population had access to electricity, leaving around

8 million citizens without access. On average, 58 percent of the urban population has access to electricity, while only about 9 percent of rural residents have it. Much of the country's electricity is imported from Ghana and Nigeria.

The West African Gas Pipeline (WAGS) delivers natural gas from the Niger River delta region in Nigeria. The 420-mile (677 km) pipeline, which began operations in 2012, runs from Nigeria to Ghana. The mostly off-shore pipeline has connections to deliver gas to Cotonou in Benin and other port cities in Togo and Ghana. The natural gas is used to produce electricity.

TOURISM

Benin's tourism industry is underdeveloped, and the government is working to build it up. In 2018, around 295,000 international visitors arrived in Benin.

Benin's president Patrice Talon speaks to members of the West African regional stock exchange (Bourse Régionale des Valeurs Mobilières) in Abidjan, Côte d'Ivoire.

This was a significant improvement over the 176,000 who came to the country in 2005.

Some of Benin's top attractions for tourists are its wildlife areas. Pendjari National Park and W National Park, both in the north of the country, are protected havens for some of Africa's most iconic creatures—elephants, lions, hippopotamuses, African buffaloes, and antelopes. In 2017, the two transnational parks were combined as an extended site, the W-Arly-Pendjari Complex, on the UNESCO World Heritage List. The parks are also home to a wide range of birds. Improved tourist facilities and access to these regions would help drive more nature tourism in Benin.

For history lovers, another top tourist site is the city of Abomey in the south. It is home to Benin's other UNESCO World Heritage site, the Royal Palaces of Abomey, which date to the 1600s. The site is a set of 10 palaces that housed the kings of Dahomey from 1625 to 1900. It includes the Historical Museum of Abomey, which relates the history of the kingdom, its desire for independence, and its resistance and fight against colonial occupation.

INTERNET LINKS

www.bbc.com/news/world-africa-50223045
This article examines the smuggling of rice and fuel across the Benin-Nigeria border.

www.heritage.org/index/country/benin
The Index of Economic Freedom assesses the economic situation in Benin.

whc.unesco.org/en/list/323
whc.unesco.org/en/list/749
These are the World Heritage listings for Benin's Royal Palaces of Abomey (*top*) and the W-Arly-Pendjari Complex (*bottom*).

www.worldbank.org/en/country/benin/overview
The World Bank provides an economic overview of Benin.

ENVIRONMENT

Agricultural workers water onion crops in Grand Popo.

5

POPULATION GROWTH AND CLIMATE change are having a detrimental effect on Benin's environment. The country is rich in wildlife, but the effects of the rising human population on the animals and plants of the region have been severe. For instance, across West Africa, more than 90 percent of the rain forest has been cut down. In Benin, as elsewhere, the forests are cleared to make more agricultural land. The plants and animals that live in the forests have been pushed into small, isolated pockets of forest that are still under threat from logging companies and even from the locals, who need firewood and meat to feed their families. Programs have been established to help alleviate the problems, but they have not come close to offsetting the rate of loss and destruction.

Some of the major environmental issues facing Benin today include water pollution and access to clean water, rampant deforestation, desertification, and illegal poaching of endangered animals.

ENDANGERED FORESTS

Deforestation is one of the leading environmental concerns in Benin. A century or so ago, southern Benin was covered in original dense forest. Today, very little of it remains. Between 1990 and 2005, the country lost 29 percent of its forest cover, or around 2,399,393 acres (971,000 ha). Those losses are probably even greater now.

In Benin's coastal regions, mangrove forests have been badly degraded. Mangroves are groups of trees and shrubs that live in dense thickets or forests along tidal estuaries; salt marshes; and other brackish, watery, or muddy coastal lands. They are important habitats for a wide range of fish and other fauna and flora, and they help protect the coasts from erosion. Mangroves also take in high quantities of carbon from the atmosphere, which helps to clean the air of carbon emissions from the burning of fossil fuels, thereby helping to alleviate the buildup of greenhouse gases that are causing climate change.

A blue-headed African jacana wades in a mangrove forest in Benin.

People take the wood from these forests for use in their cooking fires. To help alleviate the pressure on the mangrove forests, tree plantations are being established. The seedlings grow quickly into trees and are available for people to use as firewood. Also, seedlings are planted in the remainder of the mangrove forests in order to rejuvenate the area. This project is still underway.

The Niaouli and Lokoli forests are threatened by timber companies (often foreign owned) that pay the local villagers for the right to cut down the trees in their areas. These forests are home to several endangered species, including two primates: the red-bellied monkey and Geoffroy's pied colobus monkey. Many rare birds either live in these rain forests or stop there on their migrations. Protective measures such as education for local villagers and guards, as well as reforesting some areas, have resulted in the return of a few species to the forests.

Waterways of all types are in danger. Pollution in the form of unpurified sewage and urban waste, pesticides, fertilizers, and organic matter from the

Shown here is Tanongou Falls on the edge of Pendjari National Park.

RAMSAR SITES

The Ramsar Convention on Wetlands is an international treaty for the conservation and sustainable use of wetlands. The treaty dates to 1971 and is named for the Iranian city of Ramsar, where it was signed. The convention uses a broad definition of wetlands— it includes all lakes and rivers, underground aquifers, swamps and marshes, wet grasslands, peatlands, oases, estuaries, deltas and tidal flats, mangroves and other coastal areas, coral reefs, and all human-made sites such as fish ponds, rice paddies, reservoirs, and salt pans.

Wetlands are of vital importance, according to the convention, because they are among the world's most productive environments. They are ecosystems of "biological diversity that provide the water and productivity upon which countless species of plants and animals depend for survival."

As part of its mission, the convention identifies wetlands sites around the world that are of international importance and works to protect them. Of the 2,406 Ramsar sites (as of 2020), Benin has four, with a

Waterbuck antelopes graze near the Pendjari River.

combined area of 6,393,461 acres (2,587,342 ha). Two are vast coastal areas, and two are in the north—including the W National Park complex in the northeast and the humid ecosystems of the Pendjari River in the northwest. In 2019, Benin expanded and combined the two coastal Ramsar regions to include its entire coast.

coastal cities of Cotonou and Porto-Novo have led to a steady deterioration in water quality, particularly in Lake Nokoué, Benin's largest lagoon, and the Oueme River. West African manatees in those waters are hunted for their meat and are now endangered.

Manatees are mammals that look something like walruses; their forelimbs are flippers, and their hind limbs form a broad, flat paddle. The West African manatee has been the least studied of all manatee species. It lives in rivers, estuaries, and shallow coastal waters. Because this species is not well known, there are few pictures of it, and scientists know little about it but assume it to be very similar to other manatee species.

Crocodiles and sharks occasionally kill manatees, but the main threat to them is from humans, by poaching or through habitat destruction. Pollution is also a threat to the manatees, as are fishing nets—manatees need to surface to breathe air, so they will drown if caught in fishing nets. Because some manatees feed largely on mangroves, the loss of the mangrove forests is a direct threat to their survival. It is illegal in Benin to capture or kill manatees, but their population is still in decline, mostly due to loss of habitat.

A crocodile suns itself in a mangrove forest.

ENDANGERED ANIMALS

Hippos cool off in a river in Pendjari National Park.

In addition to the West African manatee, animals under threat in Benin include sea turtles, hippopotamuses, and crocodiles. The crocodiles have been threatened by cotton production because the runoff of pesticides from the cotton fields has poisoned them. Also, much of the water where they live has been pumped away to irrigate cotton fields.

The threat to the sea turtles is so great that egg nurseries have been developed to help ensure that enough turtle eggs hatch and the young turtles make it to the ocean. Also, local villagers are being educated about the importance of saving turtles and their habitat.

Another species under threat in Benin, the red-bellied guenon, is a tree-dwelling monkey that usually weighs between 4.4 pounds and 9.9 pounds (2 kilograms and 4.5 kilograms). It lives in tropical areas and prefers the wettest parts of the forest. It eats fruit, insects, and leaves. Guenons usually live in small groups of 5 to 30 individuals. In 2000, the status of this species changed from "vulnerable" to "endangered," due to a continued decline in the population because of hunting and loss of habitat. This particular species is found only in southwestern Nigeria and southern Benin, so it is very important that it is protected.

CLIMATE CHANGE

The impacts of climate change are being felt or anticipated in Benin in various ways. A projected rise in temperature and rainfall will surely affect farmers. Along the coast, where the population is most dense, rising sea levels pose an immediate threat to residents. Rising tides are eating away at coastal lands and causing massive erosion. Many homes and other structures have already been abandoned to the sea. Benin, like much of coastal West Africa, faces a high rate of coastal erosion. A study by the World Bank reported in 2019 that 65 percent of Benin's coastline has been eroding at the rate of 13 feet (4 m) a year. In addition, an increase in the frequency and violence of storms linked to climate change are adding to the toll.

West African elephants in the north of Benin are particularly vulnerable to poachers.

INTERNET LINKS

www.adaptation-undp.org/explore/western-africa/benin
This UN Climate Change Adaptation site highlights programs that are addressing climate change issues in Benin.

www.dandc.eu/en/article/deforestation-ravaging-environment-save-small-town-benin
This article focuses on the detrimental effects of deforestation in Benin.

www.ramsar.org/news/benin-extends-two-ramsar-sites-to-cover-entire-coastal-area
This is the Ramsar article about Benin's coastal wetlands.

rsis.ramsar.org/sites/default/files/rsiswp_search/exports/Ramsar-Sites-annotated-summary-Benin.pdf?1602865450
This document describes the four Wetlands of International Importance in Benin.

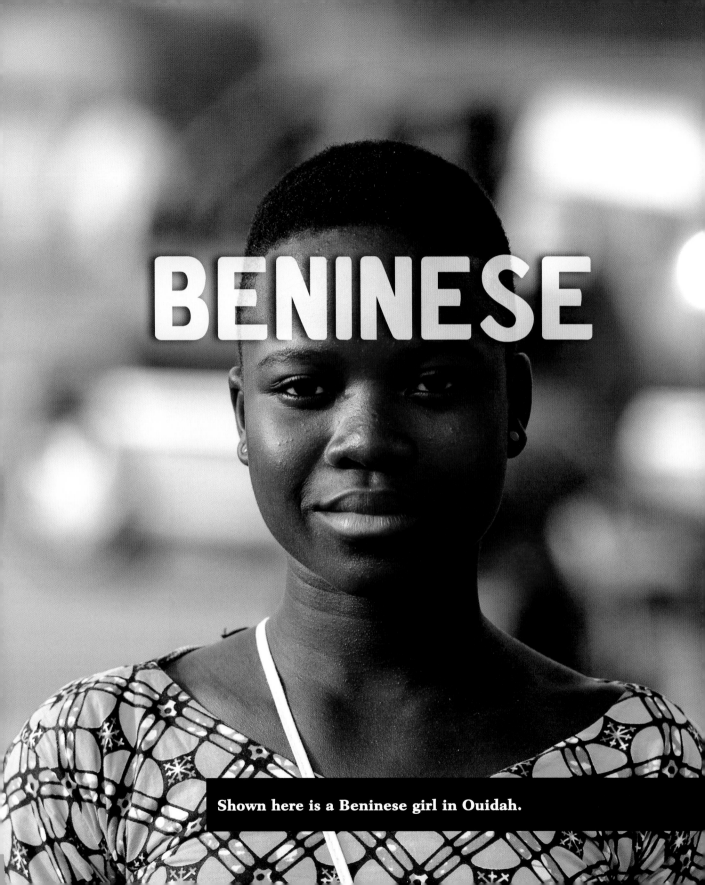

BENINESE

Shown here is a Beninese girl in Ouidah.

6

T HE PEOPLE OF BENIN ARE CALLED the Beninese. That's the English term, but they have other words for themselves. In French, the country's official language, they are the *Beninois* (Beh-neen-WAH). Most of what is known about the early history of the Beninese was passed on through oral tradition, as there were no indigenous written languages in their early history.

The approximately 12,865,000 Beninese are a mix of roughly 42 ethnic groups. The Fon people, who live mostly in the south and central areas of Benin, make up about 38 percent of the population. The Adja people, or Aja, account for about 15 percent. The Yoruba, making up about 12 percent of the people, live mainly in the southeast, and the Bariba, who make up almost 10 percent, live primarily in the north. However, there is a great deal of overlap. These people often live side by side, and their children may grow up learning several languages in addition to their own and the national language, French. With so many ethnic groups in the mix, Benin is like a quilt of many customs and traditions.

THE FON PEOPLE

Also called the Dahomey, the Fon are the largest ethnic group in Benin. The speak the Fon language and live mostly in the vicinity of Cotonou and other coastal cities and towns. They also live in Togo and Nigeria, as the boundaries of modern African nations were drawn through historic ethnic regions. Today's Fon are the descendants of those who are historically associated with the Kingdom of Dahomey. Ancestor worship remains an important element of the Fon religious tradition of Vodun. The Fon share their deep ethnic roots with the Adja people.

THE ADJA PEOPLE

The Adja people migrated into the area that is now southern Benin from the Togo region during the 12th or 13th century. The historically important three brothers who split the ruling of the region in the early 1600s were of this group. The people of the Abomey region, which became the Kingdom of Dahomey, mixed with local peoples to eventually become the Dahomey, or Fon, people.

The Adja still live primarily in the south of Benin, straddling the border with Togo, but many have migrated to southern Nigeria and Gabon. As with the Fon and other ethnic groups, there are various subgroups among the Adja, including the Aizo, the Holi, and the Mina people.

Yoruba drummers take part in a festival in Kétou.

THE YORUBA PEOPLE

The Yoruba are one of the major ethnic groups of Nigeria, Benin, and Togo. In Benin, they make up about 12 percent of the population, with most living in the southeast of the country. The Yoruba are sometimes referred to as the Nago or Nagot people in Benin.

In Yoruba tradition, their kingdoms were begun by the sons of Oduduwa. These sons came down to Earth from heaven and founded the Yoruba kingdom at Ife. Ife is in modern-day Nigeria and was a thriving city from the 12th to the 15th centuries. Even after that, when its power declined, it remained a spiritual center for the Yoruba.

Like the Fon language, the Yoruba language is a common vernacular, or home language, in Benin's southern region.

A Taneka woman sits outside a house in the village of Natitingou in northwestern Benin. The Taneka are mostly people from the Kabye, Bariba, and Gurma ethnic groups.

THE BARIBA PEOPLE

The Bariba live in central and northern Benin and are largely Muslim. They make up about 9.6 percent of Benin's population. During the 19th century, the Bariba lived in independent kingdoms such as Nikki and Kandi.

The Bariba count their descent from a legendary ancestor called Kisira. He was an Arabic warrior from the seventh century who refused to convert to Islam. He left his home in exile and traveled across Africa to found the original Bariba state at Borgou. Later, this state split into several smaller states, including Nikki, which is the dominant Bariba state in Benin. By the time of the French colonization, the Nikki dynasty had given rise to 28 kings.

After the French occupation, Nikki lost power due to its position on the extreme northern end of the colony, away from most of the trade routes.

Today, Nikki is a small town that is connected to Benin's main north-south highway by a dirt road. Although the traditional reverence connected to Nikki has faded over time, the town is still significant enough that all political candidates from the north make a point to pay their ritual respects to the king of the Bariba, who resides in Nikki.

OTHER ETHNIC GROUPS

Traditional mud and clay Somba dwellings are seen here in northern Benin.

Many ethnic groups exist in Benin, but their members are not as numerous as the Fon, the Yoruba, or the Bariba. Two of these groups are the Somba and the Fulani.

The Somba, also known as (or related to) the Tammari, Ottamari, or Ditamari, primarily live in the northwestern part of the country in the Atakora Mountains and make up approximately 8 percent of Benin's population. Mattieu Kerekou, the former president, is one of the most well-known members of this ethnic group.

They are known for their traditional body-scarring rituals, which convey lifelong identification marks on the skin. The scars are added ceremonially at various points of growth and achievement, beginning at around age 2 or 3. The Somba people are also known for their distinctive, two-story windowless houses called *Tata Somba* ("Somba house"). The lack of windows is designed to keep intruders out. Because of their houses, the Somba are sometimes called "castle peasants." The lower floor of the house is used to stable animals and for storage, while the family lives on the second floor. The Somba are mostly animist in their religion, and a shrine near the entrance of the house honors the ancestors of that family's lineage.

The soil in the area in which they live is very poor, which makes farming difficult. The Somba themselves also tend to stay isolated from others. However, to bring more income to their villages, they have begun to entice tourists to their villages during times of celebrations and dances.

The Fulani, also called Fula, Peul, or Fulbe, are found throughout West Africa. Most Fulani are Muslim. In Benin, they make up about 8.6 of the population. Traditionally, the Fulani were pastoralists—nomadic animal herders—and about a third of today's people still maintain some version of that lifestyle.

During the 19th century, the Fulani were engaged in a series of holy wars, which resulted in a far-flung but short-lived Fulani empire. Fulani legends claim they originated in Arabia and spread westward from there. The Fulani tend to be lighter-skinned than their neighbors and have thin noses and lips and slender builds.

INTERNET LINKS

africa.uima.uiowa.edu/peoples/show/Yoruba
This art history site provides information about the Yoruba people and has links to the other ethnicities in Benin (and all of Africa).

www.cia.gov/library/publications/the-world-factbook/geos/bn.html
The *World Factbook* has up-to-date statistics on demographics in Benin.

scribol.com/art-and-design/architecture-art-and-design/the-incredible-tata-somba-houses-of-west-africas-tammari-people
This site has photos of the Tata Somba buildings in the mountainous northwest.

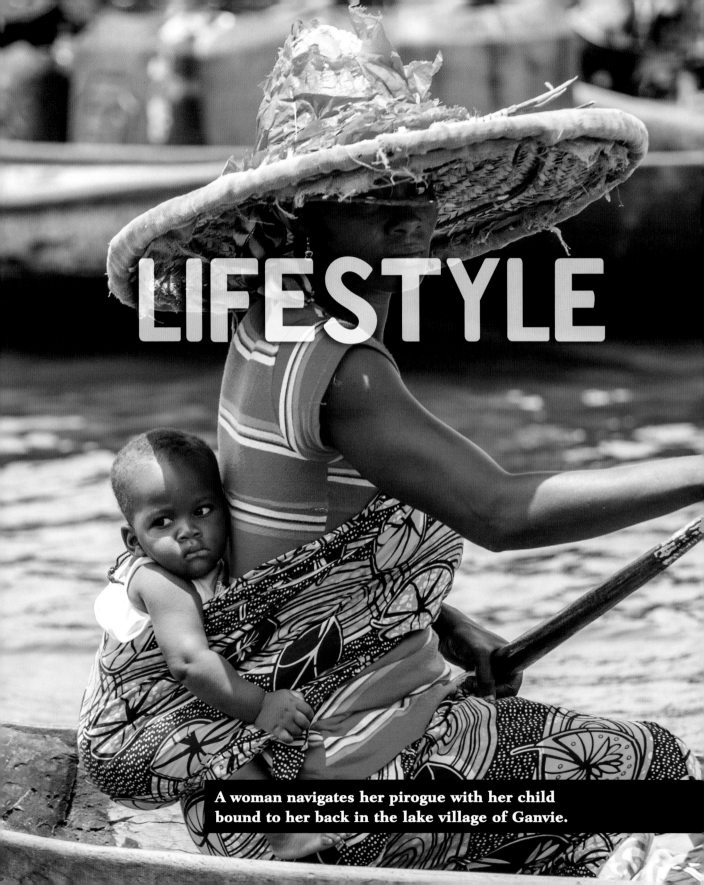

LIFESTYLE

A woman navigates her pirogue with her child bound to her back in the lake village of Ganvie.

BENINESE LIFESTYLES REFLECT A mixture of ancestral and European customs, combining the influences of history, geography, and religion. With a population representing a large number of ethnicities, many with their own distinct customs, the country has a complex and vibrant culture.

Most people in Benin live according to the traditions of their ancestors. Indeed, since their ancestors are still considered a vital part of their lives, continuing their customs is a way of showing respect. People honor their heritage, but they have also adopted some Western ways.

RURAL AND CITY LIFE

Many people in Benin live in small villages where they know everyone and follow the same traditions they have for centuries. Meals are taken on the floor, with the men separate from the women and children. Many people have radios, but many do not have electricity, running water, or indoor plumbing. Showers and toilets are located outside the house. Streets are dirt tracks through the forest or savanna and are often impassable when it rains. Most people do not own cars, but a few will operate taxis or scooters and take paying passengers along with them. Bus and postal service are somewhat regular but not always dependable.

Those who live in cities have better access to things such as electricity and indoor plumbing. They also have better access to medical care in

7

In Benin, most people live in the lower southern portion of the country. The region makes up roughly one-fourth of the country's total area but is inhabited by more than two-thirds of the total population. Nearly half (48.4 percent) of Benin's population is urban, concentrated mostly in Cotonou, the country's largest city.

Village life in Ganvie is dependent on boats.

hospitals and are more likely to be able to take a regular bus to work or the market. A higher percentage of their children will go to school and learn to read and write. Stores, gas stations, and hotels are located in the cities. Outside of the cities, people often must bring their own gas from the cities or shop at the local markets for whatever they need. Lodging is hard to come by.

People in the cities have often adopted a more Western style of dress and may eat as a family instead of eating with the men separate from the women and the children, as many do in the villages. Instead of using their hands as they eat on mats on the floor, people in the cities may use Western-style dining room furniture and utensils.

The best way to assess a nation's general health is by examining certain statistical indicators and comparing them to those of other countries. One of the primary measures used is "life expectancy at birth." This figure is the average number of years a person born in a certain year can expect to live, if mortality factors remain constant. (However, these factors don't remain constant over time, so this statistic is hypothetical.) Since this figure is an average of all life spans within a given framework, it cannot predict any specific person's length of life.

Life expectancy at birth is used to compare conditions in different countries, but it also reflects trends up or down within any given nation. Just as longer life tends to correspond to better overall health in a population, it also aligns with overall quality of life. Therefore, the statistic is valuable in determining, in general, the level of a people's living standards.

In Benin, the life expectancy in 2020 was estimated to be 61.4 years; 59.6 years for men and 63.3 years for women. This figure is very low, ranking the country at number 212 in the world, out of 228. That means people in 211 nations can expect to live longer lives than the Beninese. Their life expectancy

Beninese infants born today can expect to live around 61 years, on average.

has improved since 1960, when it was 37.27 years; but it's still a long way from Japan's 2020 expectation of 86 years.

These Beninese children help collect water from a communal well.

BIRTH AND CHILDHOOD

Children under the age of 15 make up about 45 percent of Benin's population, and the median age of the entire population is 17 years. An average Beninese woman has her first child at age 20 and has five children during her lifetime. However, because Benin is a very poor country, the resources for safe childbirth and a healthy start to life are not always available. Statistically, 405 out of 100,000 women and 56 out of 1,000 babies die in childbirth. These distressing figures are not exclusive to Benin. According to the World Health Organization (WHO), children under the age of 5 in sub-Saharan Africa are around 14 times more likely to die than children in developed regions.

Disease and malnutrition are the greatest threats. In Benin, about 40 percent of the population lives below the poverty line, and for many parents of young children, providing a balanced diet of nutritious food is simply impossible. Not surprisingly, then, nearly one-third of all Beninese children ages 6 months to 5 years suffer from chronic malnutrition, and 45 percent of all child deaths are caused by malnutrition. Underweight, malnourished children are more susceptible to disease, and in Benin, major infectious diseases such as malaria, dengue fever, diarrhea, typhoid fever, and others arise from a lack of sanitation facilities—a common consequence of widespread poverty.

Women learn to carry heavy loads, such as the harvested yams shown here, on their heads.

EDUCATION

In public schools, classes are taught in French. Native languages as well as English are taught as subjects at the secondary and university levels. Benin's literacy rate—meaning the percentage of people age 15 and over who can read and write—is very low. In 2018, the literacy rate was only 42.4 percent, with a wide discrepancy between men, at 54 percent, and women, at only 31.1 percent. Although literacy is improving in the country, these figures indicate that the education system is far from adequate.

By law, and in theory, primary school is free and compulsory from ages 6 to 11. However, that doesn't guarantee all children attend. Children in rural areas are less likely to remain in school than those in the cities. While student attendance is said to be improving, up-to-date statistics are unavailable.

In 2018, the government instituted a plan to improve its education system, to be administered through 2030. It hopes to achieve its goals with the financial help of the Global Partnership for Education, the World Bank, UNICEF, and other international support agencies. With the new Education Sector Plan, Benin

Teens in school uniforms walk along the road in Pira, Benin.

hopes to implement a 12-year universal basic education cycle, with an emphasis on reaching all children. In addition, it aims to develop a higher level of vocational training and also to improve the quality of teaching by reforming the training of teachers and administrative and guidance staff at all levels. Whether the country is able to meet these goals by 2030 remains to be seen, as there is often a big gap between political decisions and actual achievements.

HIGHER EDUCATION   Until the year 2000, there was only one university in the country, the National University of Benin. Today, that institution, based in Cotonou, is called the University of Abomey-Calavi. It is the nation's primary university and is composed of 19 institutions on 6 campuses. There are a number of other public and private institutions of higher education, and enrollment in university-level education has grown quickly. Although Benin spends more money on education than many of its neighbors—4 percent of its GDP in 2016—its resources remain limited, and the schools are plagued by problems stemming from a lack of adequate funding. Accordingly, many universities and colleges suffer from insufficient numbers of professors (classes are often overcrowded), low teaching quality, deficient infrastructure, and inadequate and outdated equipment.

MARRIAGE

As in all cultures, a wedding is an occasion for celebration. Although people in Benin have adopted some Western wedding customs, most weddings in Benin still contain some aspects of long-respected traditions.

For example, a wedding ceremony itself may be largely Western in style. The bride may wear a Western-style white dress, and the groom might wear a suit.

The ceremony usually takes place in a church with a reception following. For the reception, however, the couple will most likely have changed into traditional attire. Some Western music may be played at the reception, but traditional music is sure to be played as well.

Alternatively, however, the couple might choose to wear traditional clothing throughout. A bride might wear a *gele*, or head tie; a *buba*, or blouse; and an *iro*, which is a long piece of ankle-length fabric wrapped around her waist—along with plenty of her best jewelry. The groom might wear an *agbada*, or long caftan, of a lavish, heavy fabric, often decorated with elaborate embroidery. He would then also wear a matching headpiece. The traditional costumes differ among the various ethnic groups, but in all of them, the wedding clothing is colorful, elegant, and luxurious.

FINDING A MATCH Arranged marriages were common in the past but are less so now. However, even if a couple is more modern in the sense that they chose each other rather than allowed their families to hire a marriage broker for them, the married lifestyle tends to be very traditional. The groom will be financially responsible for the family, while the bride will be the one who takes care of the house, the children, and her husband. In the past it was common for Yoruba men, for example, to have more than one wife, but due to economic circumstances, that practice is less common today. Having large families with children very close in age has traditionally been very important to many Beninese people. However, supporting more than one household, each with its own complement of children, can be very expensive. Today, men tend to have fewer wives and fewer children by choice for practical purposes.

ENGAGEMENT RITUALS Ceremonial rituals vary among the different cultures and religions. Among the Yoruba, for instance, the prospective groom's family will meet with the prospective bride's family to officially ask permission for the daughter to marry their son. Several family members are traditionally part of this ceremony, including the prospective groom and his immediate family; the prospective bride and her immediate family; an *olopaiduro* (literally, "standing policeman"), who is a speaker appointed by the prospective groom's

Most traditions are life-affirming and joyous ways to celebrate one's heritage. However, some customs no longer fit with today's ways of thinking. One such tradition is that of child marriage, an arrangement in which one or both of the parties are under 18 years old. Almost universally, it's the bride who is still a girl, while her groom may be a much older man. This practice occurs in many cultures and countries but is particularly prevalent in sub-Saharan Africa. UNICEF, the UN humanitarian agency for children, in alignment with the UN's Convention on the Rights of the Child, considers child marriage to be a human rights violation. For the children involved, such a marriage is usually forced; girls have no say whatsoever.

In Benin, around 26 percent of females are married before their 18th birthday; 7 percent are married before the age of 15. The department supporting the most child marriages is Alibori, in the far north of the country, where 54 percent of women aged 20 to 49 were married before the age of 18. Not incidentally, the level of education in that region is extremely low.

Child marriage is driven by gender inequality and the belief that men and boys are superior to women and girls. The practice tends to go hand in hand with poverty and a lack of education. Young girls who are forced to marry usually have to drop out of school and often get pregnant before they are fully grown, which is a serious health risk. Families may choose to marry off a young daughter for several reasons. For an impoverished family, it's a way to reduce the number of mouths to feed, and the girl's father may gain financially in the exchange. Another reason, however, is because marriage is considered to be in the girl's best interest and a way of keeping her safe from harassment and sexual assault.

In 2017, Benin launched the Campaign to End Child Marriage in Africa. This project was aimed at supporting and advocating legal and policy actions in the protection and promotion of children's human rights—but also at changing minds and long-standing customs, which is not a simple task at all.

family to present their request and who may be a family member or someone hired for the occasion; and an *olopaijoko* (literally, "sitting policeman"), who represents the prospective bride's family and who may be a family member or someone they have hired for the ceremony.

This ceremony takes place at the prospective bride's house, and her family is traditionally responsible for the cost and for all preparations. If the prospective groom's family is financially able, they may volunteer to help defray the costs associated with the ceremony.

Upon entering the home, the prospective groom's female relatives kneel, and his male relatives prostrate themselves on the floor. Then, the two families sit on opposite sides of the room while the olopaiduro and olopaijoko sit in the center. The olopaiduro introduces everyone. He presents a letter from the prospective groom's family to the prospective bride's family that formally requests the woman's hand in marriage. The olopaiduro then hands the letter to the olopaijoko, who reads it out loud, and the family responds immediately. Because the families have known for some time about the young couple's wish to marry and the bride's family has made extensive preparations for this event, there is little risk of a negative answer at this stage. This is simply the time when the prospective bride's family traditionally gives their blessing for the marriage to proceed.

At this time, it is traditional for the prospective groom's family to present the bride's family with a gift (*owo-ori-iyawo*), and a prayer is offered. The olopaiduro and olopaijoko then taste several traditional foods before offering them to everyone present. When kola nuts are shared, the families repeat the words "*Won ma gbo. Won ma to. Won ma d'agba*," which means, "They will ripen. They will eat and not go hungry. They will grow old."

Also eaten are fruits called *ata ire*. These contain many seeds. According to Yoruba tradition, the number of seeds that fall from the fruit will equal the number of children the couple will have. Honey (*oyin*), sugar, and sugarcane (*ireke*) are also eaten to symbolize that the marriage will be a sweet one.

To complete the ceremony, family members may make additional speeches, and the families may exchange additional gifts. Then, it is time to eat the banquet the prospective bride's family prepared and listen to the singers and drummers who have been hired for the happy occasion.

Some time after the introduction ceremony, the couple will officially be engaged at a second ceremony. Everyone dresses in clothes made from traditional cloths called *asooke*. Once again, the families meet at the prospective bride's family's house, and her family purchases and prepares everything. Symbolic foods are presented to everyone, and gifts like a Bible or rings will be exchanged. During this ceremony, the prospective bride traditionally has her face covered.

Afterward, everyone except the prospective bride goes outside. She waits inside until she is called out. She will emerge from the house with her face still covered and kneel in front of her parents, who then offer a prayer on her behalf. After that, she will kneel before the prospective groom's parents, who also pray for her. The prospective bride then sits beside the prospective groom and removes her veil. The engagement ceremony is traditionally followed almost immediately by the wedding. After the wedding ceremony is over and the reception has been held, the bride goes to the groom's house. She is supposed to arrive first so that she can receive her husband when he arrives home.

DEATH CUSTOMS

In many Beninese communities, death marks the transition of the soul from one plane of existence to another; it is therefore greeted with rejoicing by the family, especially if the person who died was very old. Although the family is grieving, they still want to express their joy that their relative has gone on to join the rest of the ancestors. The greater the age attained before death, the greater the celebration.

If a young person dies, however, especially if they were too young to have children, the funeral will be about the loss to the family. Sometimes parents do not even attend the funeral of a child who died young. People often wish each other good fortune by saying, "May you never bury a child in your lifetime." While brighter colors may be worn at the funeral of an old person, much darker and duller colors are chosen for the burial of a young person. To show unity, the entire family may dress in clothes made from the same cloth.

It is the responsibility of the family to prepare the body for burial. In rural areas the burial is usually performed quickly after death, since there is no way to preserve a body. A man or woman whose spouse has died will cut his or her hair and will usually stay at home for a 40-day period of mourning.

In some traditions, hair and fingernail clippings are taken from the deceased person to be used in a "second burial." The second burial is performed when everyone in the family has had time to get together and prepare elaborate rituals. Because the body had to be buried quickly, there may not have been time for everyone to gather at the primary funeral. If a family anticipated a death for some time or if they are wealthy, they may have the resources to perform both burials at once. Most people must take months, or even years, to prepare the second burial properly.

At the second burial, the family wears clothing made from the same fabric. Everyone is fed and given *sodabi* (a kind of palm wine) and other beverages to drink, and musicians play all night long. People dance until the early hours of the morning.

In some traditions, it is believed the spirit of the dead person cannot move on to the land of the ancestors until the second burial is performed. The longer the family waits, the more time the unhappy spirit lingers. It may even eventually try to harm its family members if it has not been properly sent on its way. For this reason, between the first and second burials, some people wear palm fronds or place fronds over the doorways of their homes to protect them from a vengeful spirit.

INTERNET LINKS

borgenproject.org/top-10-facts-about-living-conditions-in-benin
This charitable organization lists facts about everyday life in Benin.

www.girlsnotbrides.org/child-marriage/benin
This organization provides information about child marriage in Benin and the world.

www.unicef.org/infobycountry/benin.html
UNICEF provides statistics and information relating to children in Benin.

RELIGION

A Vodun priest holds a snake at the
Temple Of Pythons in Ouidah.

8

National holidays in Benin include Christian holidays such as Christmas and Easter; Muslim holidays such as the Prophet Mohammad's birthday; and Vodun Day, January 10.

BENIN IS A RELIGIOUSLY DIVERSE nation. In most cases, religion and ethnicity go hand in hand. In the south, particularly in Cotonou, most people tend to be Christians, while most people in the north are Muslims. African traditional religions are also practiced throughout the country, with Vodun (commonly known as vodou or voodoo) being the most popular.

Vodun is an animistic religion, which means that its followers believe that every animal, plant, and thing (such as mountains, rocks, and streams) has a spirit, created by a remote, all-powerful god. Very powerful spirits can bring good or bad luck and can be influenced by prayers and sacrifices in their honor. People worship these spirits at shrines as the protectors of the natural world in which they live.

In general, about 48.5 percent of Beninese are Christians (25.5 percent Roman Catholic; 23 percent various Protestant and other Christian denominations), 27.7 percent are Muslims, 11.6 percent practice Vodun, and 11 percent have other faiths or no religion. However, these statistics are based on the 2013 census and reflect only how people self-identify. In practice, many Beninese who identify themselves as Christian or Muslim also practice Vodun or other traditional religions. Some people observe aspects of all of those faiths. A mix of faiths, cultures, and customs is called syncretism, and religions that incorporate elements from several sources are called syncretic religions.

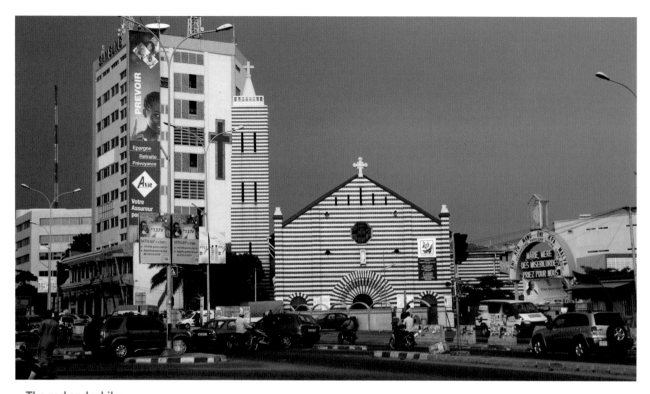

The red and white Notre Dame de Misericorde (Our Lady of Mercy) church stands at a busy intersection in Cotonou.

FREEDOM OF RELIGION

The constitution of Benin guarantees religious freedom for its citizens. Anyone wishing to form a religious group must register their group with the Ministry of the Interior. All groups must meet the same registration requirements. Tolerance between the religious communities is generally good, and interfaith dialogue is common.

Since Benin is a secular state and there is no state-sponsored religion, public schools may not provide religious instruction. However, private religious schools are allowed.

CHRISTIANITY

Christianity was originally brought to Benin by Portuguese missionaries in the 1600s. However, deaths from disease and the resistance of the locals to the missionaries' message doomed the original efforts. Only sporadic attempts—all failures—occurred over the next two centuries, but by the 1800s, they gained better footing. English Methodists arrived in 1843, and the first successful Catholic mission was established in 1860, headed by the Italian priest Francois Borghero. Catholic schools were opened at the same time. Catholicism did not reach the north of the country until 1937.

After Benin achieved independence and during its Marxist period of the 1970s and 1980s, all churches were nationalized, and missionaries were forced to leave the country. When the government changed and a new constitution was written in 1990, religious institutions were revived with new freedoms.

Most of Benin's Christians live in the south of the country. Many live in Cotonou. Most Beninese Christians belong to the Roman Catholic faith. The others belong to a variety of Christian groups such as Baptists, Jehovah's Witnesses, Assemblies of God, Seventh-day Adventists, and Mormons. Missionaries continue to operate throughout the country. Christian denominations that are known to have missionaries in Benin include the Baptists, the Church of the Nazarene, the Assemblies of God, the Mennonites, and the Mormons.

One homegrown Christian denomination, the Celestial Church of Christ (CCC), is an African initiated church (AIC), meaning it was founded independently by Africans rather than by missionaries from abroad. The Celestial Church was founded in 1947 in Porto-Novo by Samuel Bilewu Joseph Oshoffa, who claimed to have had a divine revelation. He held himself up as a prophet capable of miraculous interventions similar to those of Jesus Christ. The church's beliefs are based on the Bible but also incorporate some Muslim practices, such as separation of men and women during worship services. However, it bans all forms of African traditional practices, which are considered pagan. Today, about 6.7 percent of Beninese are members of the Celestial Church.

ISLAM

Islam arrived in Benin with Arab merchants who came across the Sahara with their goods. Thus, most of the Muslims in the country live in the north. Beninese Muslims are Sunni Muslims, one of the two main branches of the

religion and by far the most popular. The few Shia Muslims who live in Benin are generally foreigners from the Middle East.

As is true among many Christian faiths in the country, Islamic practice is often infused with Beninese culture and tradition. That is, many nominal Muslims also practice local traditional beliefs. Muslim influencers from outside the country are trying to banish those elements of African tradition and to establish a purer form of Islam in Benin.

VODUN

Every January 10 since 1992, the people of Benin have celebrated what is sometimes called their "national religion" on Vodun Day. Vodun can also be spelled "Vodoun," but it is more commonly known in the West as voodoo or vodou. The word *Vodun* means "spirit" in the Fon and Ewe languages, and the theology is focused on spirits—of nature, of deities, of dead ancestors, and of clans, tribes, and nations. This religion came to the Americas on slave ships, but it originated in the area that is now Benin and Nigeria.

People who follow Vodun may also consider themselves Catholics or Muslims, as there are some commonalities among all of the religions. Therefore, it is common for Beninese people to practice two religions without viewing them to be in conflict.

There are many versions of Vodun in Benin, but the two main ones are Vodun, practiced by the Fon people, and orisha (deity) worship, practiced by the Yoruba. For the Yoruba, the main god is Olorun, while for the Fon, the creator god is Mawu. Mawu may also be known as Dada-Segbo, Semedo, or Gbedoto, depending on the aspect of his being the person wishes to emphasize.

For instance, if one is interested in emphasizing Mawu's creation of life, he would be referred to as Gbedoto.

Priests of Vodun can be male (*houngan*) or female (*manbo*). The initiates they train to become priests are called *vodunsi*. The priest serves a particular spirit in a temple with an altar in the center. The altar can be decorated with many items, including candles, and items that represent the spirit. Several times a year, the vodunsi may go into the streets of a village, dancing to drums and wearing elaborate costumes. These ceremonies are held whenever required or wanted and do not conform to a set schedule.

Training to become a Vodun priest takes place at a special school. The students live a life of simplicity and must endure trials that test their strength and their resolve. They must memorize their lessons and repeat them back to the teachers exactly. The students must learn chants, dances, and secrets of their religion, which may not be revealed to outsiders. Other tasks for the students include making masks, baskets, and cloth, which are sold at the market. Students are not allowed to be idle; their hours are filled with work or study.

Upon graduation, the young priests are urged to be responsible to the land, the spirits, their ancestors, and their fellow priests. Each is given a handful of sand from his or her native land to emphasize where his or her responsibilities lie.

Vodun encompasses magic, both good and bad. Good magic (*bo*) exists in the form of spells or charms that turn away evil. Evil magic (*aze*) harms people. Sorcerers who practice evil sorcery are despised.

DIVINATION AND INITIATION

According to Vodun beliefs, each person has a destiny attached to them before birth. The Fon call this *fa*, and the Yoruba call it *ori*. People must go to a diviner to discover this destiny. The diviner is called *bokono* by the Fon and *babalao* by the Yoruba. A person who has a question about their life, past, present, or future, can go to a diviner, who will throw seed pods or cowrie shells to find the answers. Spirits supposedly control the way the pods or shells fall so that the diviner can read the message that the spirits want conveyed.

THE VODUN AND ORISHA

The supreme god of Vodun and orisha worship is considered to be too infinite and remote for ordinary human beings to deal with, and this god is not actually worshiped. For their needs, humans must appeal to and appease spirits closer to hand. These spirits were created by the supreme being and are above all natural laws; their responsibilities include interacting with humans. They are the ones to receive worship from living people. They have nothing to do with the dead, except to deliver their souls to the creator god.

People worship thousands of spirits, but the seven most important in Vodun, all considered sons of Mawu, are the following:

- *Sakpata, the eldest son, who has been given lordship over the earth. People are afraid of him because of his terrible power. Symbols of his power include scissors, chains, and smallpox. He has many sons, including Ada Tangni, the spirit of leprosy, and Sinji Aglosumato, the spirit of incurable sores.*

- *Xevioso is the lord of the sky and of thunder. He is responsible for punishing liars and criminals. His symbols include a double-headed axe, lightning, fire, and the color red.*

- *Agbe is lord of the sea. His symbol is a serpent.*

- *Gu (or Ogun) is lord of war and iron. He is responsible for giving technology to people, as well as for punishing accomplices to doers of evil deeds.*

- *Age is lord of agriculture, animals, and forests.*

- *Jo is invisible and is lord of the air.*

- *Legba is the youngest son. After his other brothers were given lordship over various things, nothing was left over for him. Legba was jealous of his brothers and became the spirit of unpredictability.*

In orisha worship, some of the main spirits worshiped are Shango, a sky spirit who rules storms and lightning; Erinle, the spirit of the forest; Agwe, the spirit of the ocean; Oko, the spirit governing agriculture; and Ezili, the spirit of love. The most popularly worshiped of these is Shango because he is believed to be the father of the Yoruba themselves. Shango's symbols are a double-headed axe and the color red, so he is very similar in that respect to the Fon god Xevioso.

Initiation into the religion is gradual and takes place at various times during a person's life. Shortly after birth, a child will be presented to the family and community (this includes the deceased ancestors) in a ceremony called *agabasa-yiyi*. The name of this ritual consists of the words for the front room of the house, *agbasa*, and the word for receiving or reception, *yiyi*. At this ceremony the diviner will reveal the destiny of the child, as well as the *joto* (deceased ancestor) whose personality animates the child. This joto is not a spirit because the dead ancestors have gone on to another realm, called *Yesunyime*. However, an aspect of the personality of the dead is left behind, to continue to live from family member to family member in the form of their joto. This joto will be the protector (*se*) of the child. Once the joto is recognized, it is welcomed back to the family with the phrase "*Se doo nu we*" ("Se, we welcome you").

The *du* ("the word of the oracle") is entrusted to the parents, especially the mother, to keep for the child until he or she is older. Each du has its own particular rules that must be followed. For instance, a du may forbid certain foods to be eaten, so the mother would not fix those foods for the children with that du, but when they are older, around 12 or 13, the children would be informed of their du and held responsible for avoiding these foods themselves. At that age, children are considered *do so kan nu*, or mature enough to take on the responsibility for their own destiny.

The agabasa-yiyi ritual is extremely important. It ties the baby not only to their living family but also to the ancestors who have gone before and to the du that will govern and direct his or her life. Those who have never had this ritual performed for them do not have status in the community. Without du and joto to tie them to the living, the dead, destiny, and the community at large, they are people without roots. If people suspect that someone has not gone through this ritual, they will feel compelled to inquire whether or not it has been performed.

At around the age of 20, men and women are initiated into another stage of Vodun through a ritual called *fa-sinsen* or *fa-yiyi*, the receiving of the fa. Young people are presumed to be troubled by their fa and must make a public declaration of their reception and devotion to it in order to find personal harmony; youthful rebelliousness and freedom come under adult self-control. Once again, a diviner is consulted, and this time an animal is sacrificed in order to clear the young person's path of obstacles and misfortunes.

A third initiation is available only to men. It is called *fa-tite*, or the consultation of the fa. A candidate applies for a consultation in order to receive the entire revelation of his destiny. This initiation ceremony takes place in the forest and cannot be observed by women or non-initiated men. The diviner once again throws nuts or shells in order to discover what knowledge the spirits have to pass on concerning the initiate. If the signs are positive, everyone present rejoices. If the signs are negative, animals are sacrificed in order to ward off the death, illness, poverty, and despair that may be coming to the individual as part of his destiny. The initiate takes a bath in flowing water to cleanse himself after the ceremony, and parts of his body, such as bits of hair and fingernails, are buried in the forest to symbolize the initiate's desire to cast away impurity. After this, the initiate goes home confident he knows the meaning of his own life, his own personal destiny having been completely revealed.

The annual Vodun festival in Ouidah attracts about 10,000 people.

Olokun is an orisha spirit widely worshiped in West Africa who may be male, female, or androgynous (a combination of male and female), depending on the culture. Among the Yoruba, Olokun is female and is the wife of Olorun, the creator god. She is the mother of all bodies of water.

Olokun rules over history, the future, visions, patience, and endurance. This spirit is also responsible for material wealth and mental health and is especially concerned with women who desire children. Because Olokun has governance over the ocean, those who were taken away during the slave trade are thought to be under the spirit's patronage. Olokun works closely with Oya, the spirit of sudden changes, and with ancestors to help people negotiate the transition between life and death. Politicians often gravitate to Olokun, as this spirit is responsible for helping people rise in political and social spheres.

An example of a prayer to Olokun is as follows:

> *"I praise the spirit of the vast ocean;*
> *I praise the spirit of the ocean who is beyond understanding;*
> *Spirit of the ocean, I will worship you as long as there is water in the sea;*
> *Let there be peace in the ocean, let there be peace in my soul.*
> *Spirit of the ocean, ageless one, I give respect. May it be so."*

SHRINES

Humans communicate with the divine in Vodun or orisha worship through shrines. Shrines come in many forms. They may be something natural, such as a clearing in a forest or a tree, or they can be something man-made, such as a building or a stick poked into the ground. The landscape of the entire country is filled with such shrines, which people have set aside and erected to ensure that they have the ability to reach the spirits.

The shrine is the point where two worlds—the world of spirits and the world of people—meet. At its spiritual center is an altar where people will place sacrifices, such as alcohol, money, or food. People may do this for their personal benefit or may gather as families or communities in order to worship and petition for the things they desire.

WITCHES AMONG THE BARIBA

Despite their conversion to Islam, many Bariba believe in sorcery. They will protect their children from evil spells by using amulets, such as strings or waistbands, or folk medicines. The Bariba keep a wary eye out for several kinds of magic and folk illnesses. One of the things they are most concerned about is the presence of witch children among them.

Babies who are believed to be born as witches are referred to as biiyondo. *The Bariba believe that witches are simply born witches and cannot help who they are. Their very presence will cause bad things to happen to the people around them due to their inborn evil power. Babies who are believed to be born witches may be discovered by such signs as breech birth, being born with teeth, having their teeth first erupt in the upper jaw, being born too early, or having birth defects. In the past, children who were believed to be born witches were killed by a local specialist or through parental neglect.*

When modern clinics were first established in the Bariba area, many women refused to give birth there because they would not have the same control that they would at home. In the clinics, the women could not be assured that the medical staff would recognize the signs of a witch birth or would do what was "necessary" to dispose of the witch. Women feared being sent home with a witch child.

Although laws were passed making home births illegal, many women preferred to pay the fine and give birth at home. As clinic births become more common, though, new rituals have been conceived that promise to neutralize the witch baby's power without killing the child. The neutralization requires herbs and fumigation, but many people do not have any faith that such spells will work. Therefore, such babies are still in danger of being abandoned or killed. Sometimes, because missionaries are willing to take in abandoned children, the infants are left at the missions.

One ritual that often takes place at shrines is spiritual possession. Worshipers believe they are possessed by spirits. Others may then have the opportunity to talk to the spirit directly through the medium of the possessed person.

Sometimes worshipers prefer certain kinds of shrines over others. Among the Yoruba, the shrines of the god Ogun, who is lord of war, iron, and hunting, are often based around living trees that have the lower branches trimmed away. A woven garment like a skirt is placed onto the tree; it is called "the dress of Ogun." At the base of the tree, iron staffs are driven into the ground, since this is the metal sacred to the god. Smaller shrines not placed around trees may simply be two pieces of iron driven into the ground. The shrine becomes sacred when palm oil is poured onto it.

Rituals to Ogun often involve iron bells and machetes, which are used during his ceremonies and, when not in use, can be seen near the shrine. Ogun represents both destructive and creative forces. To appease his destructive nature, which is symbolized by the color red, people offer Ogun sacrificial blood, usually from the animals sacred to Ogun: the tortoise, the snail, and the dog. To appeal to Ogun's creative side, worshipers offer palm wine. By doing these things, people hope to keep destructive forces from entering their own lives, especially through any sort of industry or accident involving cars, guns, knives, mechanical equipment, or anything else made of metal.

Though many Beninese have converted to Islam or Christianity, they also often practice some form of native religion such as Vodun or orisha worship. These religions are central to people's lives. By worshiping and offering sacrifices to the spirits, these people express a spirituality and depth of faith that helps them cope with a complicated and rapidly changing world.

INTERNET LINKS

www.bbc.com/news/world-africa-15792001
This quick article provides a look at Vodun (voodoo) in Benin.

www.globalsecurity.org/military/world/africa/bn-religion.htm
A general overview of religion in Benin includes a focus on Vodun.

www.nytimes.com/2012/02/05/travel/on-the-vodun-trail-in-benin.html
This travel article provides a close-up look at Vodun practices in Benin.

www.state.gov/wp-content/uploads/2020/06/BENIN-2019-INTERNATIONAL-RELIGIOUS-FREEDOM-REPORT.pdf
This is the U.S. Department of State report on religious freedom in Benin.

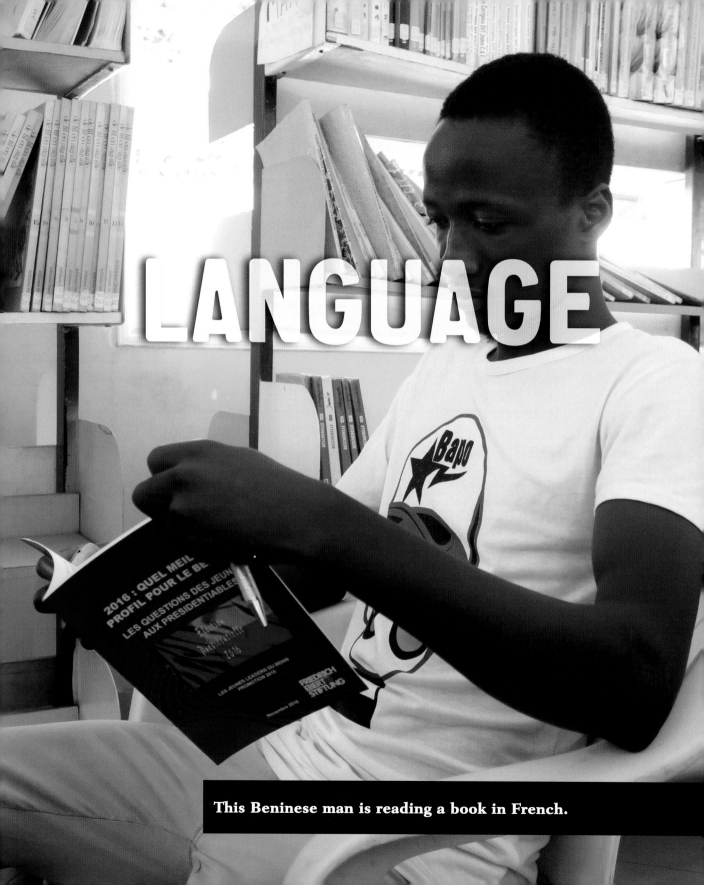

LANGUAGE

This Beninese man is reading a book in French.

MANY LANGUAGES ARE SPOKEN IN Benin, and among those, there are many dialects. In order for people to communicate beyond the boundaries of their home villages, therefore, it's necessary for there to be a *lingua franca*, or one language that people have in common. French is the official language—a remnant of its colonial occupation—and it is taught in the schools. French is used in all government documents and proceedings. All print media is in French, and people who seek jobs in the cities have a better chance of being hired if they speak French.

However, not all Beninese speak French; in fact, only about 35 percent or so do. Around their own villages, people speak their native languages. These languages, like many in Africa, are tonal, which means that the tone with which words are spoken influences the meaning. This is very difficult for speakers of English to learn, as English is not tonal.

As education and literacy improves in Benin, there will be a higher percentage of French speakers.

9

There are 53 different dialects of the Fon language spoken throughout Benin.

A man reads newspaper headlines on the streets of Cotonou.

FON

Fon is the most popular of the native languages; it's spoken primarily in the south and southeast parts of Benin. Fon is also called Fongbe, meaning "Fon language" and is a member of a language family called Gbe, which also includes the languages of the Ewe and the Adj. In turn, the Gbe languages are part of the Niger-Congo family of languages, which are spoken all across West Africa. Tradition claims that Gbe speakers originated much farther east than their present-day locations in Benin and Togo, but that Yoruba attacks between the 10th and 13th centuries sent them fleeing westward. Gbe speakers then founded the kingdom of Tado, which today would be located in the country of Togo. Other Gbe speakers left Tado to form other kingdoms in later centuries, including the kingdom of Allada, which for a time was the capital of the Fon people.

By 1850, missionaries brought Christianity to the area. These missionaries began to produce dictionaries and grammar books that recorded many local dialects of the Gbe languages. Though they were not without mistakes, these efforts began to display the wealth of languages and dialects the area nurtured. Since then, many scholars have advanced the West's knowledge of the Gbe languages.

Gbe languages have several things in common. Perhaps the strangest thing for speakers of English or other European languages is that Gbe languages, like all other native Benin languages, are tonal. Most of them display three tones: high, mid, and low, although in many dialects the lower two are not differentiated by native speakers. Tonal languages use the pitch of the word to convey its meaning. Thus two words may be spelled the same and pronounced the same but have different pitches, and so are different words with different meanings.

Children learn the tones of their native language by copying the adults around them. Interestingly, children often learn the tones of their language before anything else. Speakers of non-tonal languages who attempt to learn a tonal language as adults may have a great deal of trouble in hearing and interpreting the different tones.

In tonal languages, the pitch rather than the stress on the word and its syllables may change or subtly shift its meaning. In Igala, a tonal language of Nigeria, the word *awo* can mean "to slap," "guinea fowl," "hole in a tree," "comb," "star," or "increase," depending on tone.

Gbe languages generally have a sentence structure similar to that of English, with the basic sentence being subject-verb-object, as in, "The boy threw the ball." When it comes to verb tense, however, Gbe languages are different from English, distinguishing only between present and future. Past tense must be understood through context or by the placement of special adverbs that describe the definite end of an action.

Questions in Gbe languages often require what is called a question marker. This is a special word that changes the sentence from a statement to a question. In Fon, this is a final *a* added to the end of the question. "*A se Fongbe a*?" means "Do you speak Fon?"

Banners welcome visitors to Cotonou in both French and English.

YORUBA

Yoruba is a language spoken mostly along Benin's eastern border with Nigeria. Most, though not all, of its 300 dialects are spoken in Nigeria. It is part of the Benue-Congo branch of the Niger-Congo language family. Yoruba is tonal like the Gbe languages. In Yoruba, the word *igba* might mean "half a calabash," "two hundred," or "locust tree," depending on tone.

When greeting others in Yoruba, it is important to note the relative age of the person to whom one is speaking. For example, people use one greeting for those who are the same age or younger than themselves, but a different one for someone older. When saying "good morning" to someone the same age or younger, the phrase would be "*kuaro*;" while to someone older, the phrase used would be "*e kuaro*."

Not all phrases have two forms, however. Sometimes the same phrase will be used no matter the age of the person. For instance, "goodbye" is always *odabo*, "yes" is always *be ni*, "no" is always *oti*, and "good night" is always *o di aro*.

BARIBA

Bariba is a language in the north of Benin, and it is also spoken by people in parts of western Nigeria. It belongs to the Gur, or Savannas, branch of the Niger-Congo language family.

Some words in Bariba are:

Baaba	Father
Mero	Mother
Yaburu	Market
Wuu	Village
Ka weru	Greetings
Oh	Response to *ka weru*
A bwan do?	How are you?
Alafia	Fine
N kwaweru	Until we meet again

NAMES

In Benin, as in many places, the naming of a child is not just a random matter. It has great importance in terms of family, culture, ethnicity, and language. Here are some examples.

NAMING A FON CHILD   As soon as a Fon woman knows she is pregnant, she will take note of significant events in her life and weigh what they might mean in relation to the baby and the name he or she should have. Even small events such as whom she meets in the market or whom she speaks with when she fetches water could be important.

Newborns are examined for things like birthmarks or deformities, the position in which they exited the womb is noted, and even whether they cry

is important enough to take note of. Children may be named after the day of the week on which they were born, by some attribute they were born with, or by birth order.

Sometimes the circumstances of labor and delivery are important. If a woman goes into labor on her way to the market, she might name her child Alifoe ("man of the road") or Alipossi ("girl of the road").

NAMING A BARIBA CHILD Newborn children are immediately given a name that represents their place in the family, for instance first daughter or third son, and they may be given a Muslim name when they are 8 days old. However, it is not until the child is 4 or 5 years old that he or she receives their own name. Children lack the ability to reason, and so their entry into Bariba society follows a progression rather than happening all at once at birth.

NAMING A YORUBA CHILD   Parents may name their child after his or her father's occupation or the circumstances of the birth. A hunter, who uses equipment like a gun or spear made of iron, may name a child Ogunbunmi, which means "Ogun (the god of iron) gave me this." The firstborn of twins may be named Taiwo ("taster of the world"), while the secondborn may be named Kehinde ("late arrival"). The traditional name for a child born to a mother who has had a pair of twins is Idowu, and the child born after that may be named Alaba if it is a girl or Idogbe if it is a boy. A baby born in the breech position may be named Ige, while the names Ojo (for a boy) and Aina (for a girl) are traditional for babies born with the umbilical cord wrapped around the neck. A child born with curly hair might be named Dada.

Children may be named after the day of the week on which they were born, or they may be named Abiodun (if born on a festival day) or Bosede (if born on a holy day). If a female family member died shortly before the birth of a girl, the child may be named Yetunde ("she has come back"). If a male family member had died shortly before the birth of a boy, the baby may be named Babatunde ("he has come back"). Another traditional name is Tokunbo, which signifies that the parents were out of the country when the child was born.

INTERNET LINKS

nalrc.indiana.edu/doc/brochures/fon.pdf
This National African Language Resource Center brochure provides some information about the Fon people and their language.

omniglot.com/writing/bariba.htm
omniglot.com/writing/fon.htm
omniglot.com/writing/french.htm
omniglot.com/writing/yoruba.htm
Omniglot provides an introduction to these and other Beninese languages.

ARTS

Artwork stands in a park in Cotonou.

10

I N BENIN, THE ARTS ARE VERY MUCH A part of daily living, rather than merely the content of museum collections. That doesn't mean the culture has not produced many museum-worthy objects— it definitely has, and these artworks are exhibited at international galleries the world over. However, the traditional arts of Benin—such as storytelling, weaving, and music—are integral to the festivals, religious observances, and leisure activities of everyday life.

• • • • • • • • • • • • •
The arts of the
Kingdom of Dahomey
more properly
represent the
peoples of today's
Republic of Benin
than the arts of the
Kingdom of Benin,
which was in
today's Nigeria.

MUSIC

Modern musical genres such as jazz, reggae, R'n'B, rock, funk, and hip-hop are all popular in Benin. Traditional music, however, has the deepest roots.

Among the Yoruba, the most important traditional musical instruments are the drums. An iron bell may be used in music dedicated to Ogun, the spirit of iron, and a gourd rattle is often added to music dedicated to the spirit of thunder. For the most part, though, drums make up the music of the Yoruba.

One form of music is the *bata* ensemble. Several kinds of drums make up the ensemble. They are the *omeleako* ("male small drum"), the

omele abo ("female small drum"), the *eki*, and the *iyailu* ("mother drum"). The first three perform most of the structure of each piece, while the mother drum plays a different but supporting rhythm. The omeleako may interact with the rest of its section or change to match the mother drum at times.

Yoruba in other countries and their descendants in the Americas have similar ensembles, but the Benin bata groups are unique. Their iyailu and omeleako have much lower pitches than those of drums in Nigeria or Brazil. Also, the eki is not used elsewhere.

Bata ensembles are used during Egungun rituals. During a ceremony, the *elegun* (initiates) begin dancing in the afternoon around a tree where three bata players are located. Male dancers form an outer circle, and female dancers form an inner circle. Women dance with bodies leaning forward and arms down, taking small steps to the rhythm of the drums. Men dance with longer

Benin's most famous international music star is Angelique Kidjo. She is not only a singer-songwriter but also an actor and a human/women's/children's rights and peace activist. She is also active in environmental and climate change campaigns.

Angelique Kidjo performs in concert at Jazzopen, an annual summer jazz festival in Stuttgart, Germany.

Born in Ouidah just two weeks before her country became independent, she calls herself a "daughter of independence." She is fluent in five languages—French, English, and three native languages of Benin: Fon, Yoruba, and Gen, a Gbe language—and sings in all of them. Kidjo began singing at a young age and had early success in western Africa. In 1983, during the difficult Marxist regime in her country, she moved to Paris. There, she continued her music study and performance, and she became locally quite popular. In 1991, she was signed to Island Records, which brought her to international attention, and in 2000, she recorded two albums for Columbia Records.

To date, she has released at least 17 albums, numerous singles, and videos. Kidjo has performed all over the world, with top artists from many cultures. The list of her awards is seemingly endless. Four of her albums have won Grammy Awards, including Djin Djin *(2008),* Eve *(2015),* Sings *(2016), and* Celia *(2020).*

strides and lift their arms to touch their hands over their heads, then let their arms fall down to their sides with a loud slap. Sometimes the men dance more acrobatically, guided by the drums. The rhythm of the drums is short, sharp, and strident in order to remind people of the nature of the spirits.

Another sort of drumming group is the *dundun* ensemble, which in Benin is often referred to as *gangan*. This ensemble contains an iyailu solo bass drum, which for this ensemble is called a dundun drum. It is an hourglass-shaped instrument. The membranes of the drum are pierced by a leather string, which the musician can use to change the tension in the drum. In other ensembles, the iyailu also has strings, but they are left free. Another drum in this ensemble is the *kerikeri*, which has a higher pitch and is played by being struck with either a hand or a stick. The other drums in this ensemble are the *omele*, the *asasu*, and *gudugudu*. The gudugudu has only one membrane and is played with two small leather sticks.

Music is an integral part of daily life in Benin and is indispensable during rituals for Vodun and orisha worship. The instruments have their own sounds, names, and parts to play in the various ensembles that make up Benin's musical tradition.

WEAVING

Textiles have always been central to much of Yoruba social and religious life. The Yoruba tell the story of how, in the beginning, people went about naked and were always arguing. The spirit Eshu decided to do something about that, so he taught men to harvest cotton, weave it into cloth, and wear it. When the other people saw the cloth, they responded with respect, and social harmony came to people for the first time.

Women used an upright loom to make a traditional indigo-and-white striped cloth called *kijipa*. In the past, a woman would recruit her sisters and daughters to help her spin the thread to be used in the loom. Kijipa cloth was widely traded to the north via overland routes and to Europeans on the coast who sold them in the Gold Coast (modern-day Ghana), the Congo, and Brazil.

Other ceremonial cloths were made in local patterns and styles using the upright loom. If the cloth was particularly important to certain rituals, a man

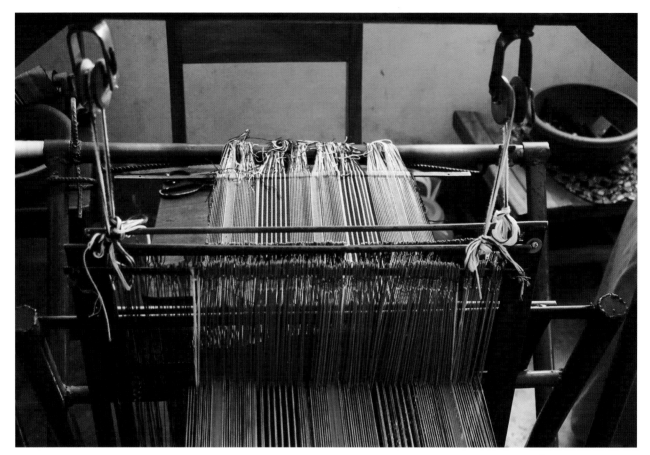

might have woven it, though men did not generally use the upright loom. Today, few weavers of either gender still use the upright loom.

Most of the cloth woven by men is produced on a narrow-strip loom that was originally imported into the Yoruba region from the north via the overland trade routes. Today, the colors and styles of the Yoruba weavers reflect recent fashions, but three traditional cloths are still made. They are *etu*, *sanyan*, and *alaari*. Together, these traditional cloths of the Yoruba are referred to as asooke. Ritual cloths like asooke are worn for weddings, birthdays, a baby's naming ceremony, engagements, funerals, and religious festivals.

Etu cloth is of a blue that is so dark that the threads used to weave it had to be immersed many times in the indigo dye. The dark color is offset by lighter threads that make stripes sometimes only one thread in width. Etu means "guinea fowl," and the cloth is supposed to resemble the speckled

Shown here is handmade cotton cloth on a loom.

VODUN ART

The religious art of Vodun is seen in the statues, masks, and costumes used in traditional rituals.

Bocio, seen below, are carved wooden statues depicting supernatural beings and are thought to hold powerful magical forces. The word means "empowered (bo) cadaver (cio)" in the Fon language of Benin. Typically, the artifacts are packed with medicines and other objects, and they are bound in chains or tied with ropes to hold the magic inside. Bocio are made to be deliberately frightening or repulsive—or counter aesthetic, the opposite of what the maker considers beautiful or pleasing. The object's power, when summoned through ritual, helps protect the person who owns it.

Murals in Vodun temples are colorful depictions of gods and spirits. Cyprien Tokoudagba was a well-known Beninese sculptor and Vodun temple painter whose work depicts symbolic, otherworldly images of religious and cultural motifs, such as hybrid animal-human creatures.

feathers of the bird. A person who wears etu is one who is well respected, and there is a Yoruba proverb saying that a man who wears an etu-cloth cap on his head will never again have to carry anything for himself.

Sanyan cloth is beige and is made from the silk of the Anaphe moth. The silk is undyed, so the beige color can be uneven. The final cloth often has a white stripe in the center of each woven strip.

Alaari cloth is made using a magenta-dyed silk imported from across the Sahara. Because it had to be imported over a great distance, this cloth was always extremely rare, and entire outfits of it were rarer still. Usually, small bits of alaari would be used as stripes in a cloth produced locally.

One shift that has occurred during the past century is that the consumers for asooke are no longer the royal and other important families but rather the educated elite of the cities. They set a fashion still popular today, in which groups of people at celebratory events express their unity by wearing outfits in the same cloth. The demand for asooke has meant a revitalization of the weaving industry and has required so many weavers that women have joined the men as producers of asooke.

The braiding of sleeping mats is an art in Benin.

LITERATURE AND PHILOSOPHY

The oral tradition, with its storytelling griots, is Benin's deeply-rooted literary heritage. Folk tales passed wisdom and values from generation to generation as they explained the peoples' understanding of their world in preliterate times. Today, these stories are rich with cultural significance, myths, and lore. Modern griots perform at festivals and in storytelling contests.

Raouf Mama is an English professor in Connecticut who has worked to get the folktales of his native Benin into print. He has worked with UNICEF and the School of African Heritage to promote cultural awareness through storytelling and has authored several books of tales, including *Why Goats*

Benin's coastal location as a historical departure point for the transatlantic slave trade led to that portion of the West African coast being called the Slave Coast. Today, that devastating history is memorialized in Benin's former slave port, Ouidah, with a memorial called the Door of No Return.

The arch, which was built in 1995, stands on a sandy beach and looks out to the Atlantic Ocean. The view is a somber reminder of the vast unknown faced by the more than 1 million enslaved African people who left these shores against their will. A mural at the top of the arch shows lines of chained people walking to a ship at sea (above). The memorial was built as part of the Slave Route Project, a creative collaboration between the Beninese government and UNESCO in the early 1990s. The project produced a series of statues, monuments, and art installations commemorating the massive and monstrous slave trade that dominated the region from the early 16th to the late 19th century.

At times, the port of Whydah (today's Ouidah) exported around 1,000 enslaved people a month. In 1860, the last recorded shipment of enslaved Africans to the United States left from Whydah, even though the United States had prohibited the transatlantic slave trade in 1808. The illegal shipment was sent aboard the Clotilda *and disembarked in Mobile, Alabama.*

Smell Bad (1998) and *Why Monkeys Live in Trees* (2006). In 2014, he published his memoir, *Fortune's Favored Child*.

Another Beninese who has had a varied career as an author, philosopher, and politician is Paulin J. Hountondji. He was born in 1942 and educated in Paris. After he earned his doctorate, he took teaching jobs in France and other parts of Africa, but within a few years he was offered a job at the National University of Benin in Cotonou, where he still teaches today.

Much of Hountondji's works center on the nature of African philosophy. One of his books was placed on a list of Africa's 100 best books of the 20th century. That book was *Sur la "Philosophie Africaine,"* which was originally published in 1976. An English translation was published in 1983 under the title *African Philosophy: Myth and Reality.*

Other well-respected Beninese writers include writer, journalist, and magazine editor Olympe Bhely-Quenum, short story writer Florent Couao-Zotti, playwright Jean Pliya, novelist Adelaide Fassinou, feminist poet Colette Sénami Agossou Houeto, children's writer Béatrice Lalinon Gbado, and many others.

INTERNET LINKS

www.atlasobscura.com/places/door-of-no-return
This article provides a look at the Door of No Return memorial in Ouidah.

www.kidjo.com
Angelique Kidjo's official site presents a biographical overview and discography.

theculturetrip.com/north-america/usa/new-york/new-york-city/articles/cyprien-tokoudagba-s-voodoo-visions-benin-conte
This quick article presents some of the works of Cyprien Tokoudagba.

www.theguardian.com/world/gallery/2020/jan/12/benin-celebrates-west-african-voodoo-in-pictures
Vodun art is shown in photos in this article about a festival in Porto-Novo.

LEISURE

A boy plays football (soccer) with bare feet in Bohicon, Benin.

11

FOR MOST PEOPLE IN BENIN, LEISURE time is spent simply. Visiting family or friends and resting at home with the radio or TV on are well-earned pleasures. People play traditional games, such as *oware*—which is similar to Mancala—and checkers, or active outdoor games, such as soccer. People of all ages always enjoy the arrival of a traveling theater troupe or a storyteller.

Children get up at dawn with their families and do their chores. Girls usually have many more chores than boys. Girls are responsible for sweeping the floor, helping with the laundry, taking care of younger siblings, and fetching water, as well as going to school, assuming their families want them to be in school. Boys are responsible for their schoolwork but otherwise often get to play soccer or other games with their friends.

A Beninese childhood is often influenced by poverty, and children must resort to their own creativity. They often make their own toys out of items they find, such as old tin cans, pieces of wood, or string. Sharing toys is an important part of growing up. A child may have a ball, a doll, or a hoop and a stick with which to roll it. Otherwise, they have very little that American children would recognize as toys.

Leisure activities differ in urban and rural environments. People who live in Benin's major cities have opportunities to attend concerts, sports events, festivals, and museums that are less often found in the rural regions. Regardless of where they live, however, most Beninese don't have much money to spend on leisure.

SPORTS

One thing that brings Beninese of all ethnicities and religions together is their love for football (or what Americans call soccer). Football is the most popular sport in Benin, but tennis is loved as well. The national football team is called Les Ecureuils ("The Squirrels"), and their home stadium is Stade de l'Amitie ("Friendship Stadium") in Cotonou. Although the team has never made it to the World Cup championships, it has qualified several times for the Africa Cup of Nations tournament.

Benin regularly sends athletes to the Summer Olympic Games but has yet to win a medal as of 2020.

Soccer is a very popular game for kids in Benin.

An outdoor market
in Cotonou attracts
a crowd
of shoppers.

THE MARKET

In Benin, many people travel to markets to find what they need. At a market, one can find nearly anything: pots, pans, shoes, spices, crocodile skins, monkey skulls, and even chicken feet! Many vendors offer items for use in home devotions to the gods of Vodun or orisha worship, while others sell household items. Especially useful are sandals made from old tires. The rubber from the tires is too thick for thorns to puncture, so the farmers who wear the sandals will not have their feet pierced while working in the fields.

Women who sell goods in the market may walk many miles before dawn to set up their stalls. They carry their goods on their heads, and any small children they have who cannot be left at home will be strapped to their backs.

Clothing is rarely sold at the market, but cloth is readily available. Most people buy cloth and then make their own clothes or hire a seamstress or a tailor to make the clothes.

THEATER

People enjoy the antics of traveling theater troupes. When the troupe visits a village, the performers, as all visitors are expected to do, visit the chief's house for his blessing. Once that is secured, the troupe will go to an open area near the village center or market and hang the curtains that divide the stage from the backstage areas. If they have modern equipment such as microphones or lights, the performers will also set those up.

Meanwhile, a griot, or traditional storyteller, travels around the village, playing on his drums. People know that means a theatrical performance is imminent. In the next hour or so, people arrive at the village center, looking for the area where the troupe has set up the equipment.

When the play is to start, the griot begins setting the scene by spinning the tale. Eventually, the actors take over and perform the rest of the play.

Most small villages do have radios but do not have access to television and movies, and most people cannot read. Therefore, a traveling troupe coming into the village to perform a play is very popular, and everyone who can attend will.

GRIOTS

Griots can be found across West Africa. They are professional entertainers who keep the oral history and genealogy of their region alive. Traditionally, many ceremonies and rituals require the attendance of a griot to provide the music. Before a wedding, a griot will come to sing to the bride about her new life and reassure her that if her marriage is terrible, she can come home.

Because their training is oral, a griot must spend many years as an apprentice to a professional. This teacher is usually a father or an uncle. In this way, the oral traditions and songs of a region are passed down through the generations. Griots are paid by those who hire them, but the payment is not set, and a griot will never exactly know what he might receive as payment. Perhaps it will be cash, or a blanket, or food.

Good griots have fantastic memories and can recall long genealogies or vast quantities of local history at a moment's notice. Sometimes a griot will have memorized the genealogies of everyone in a village going back 100 or 200 years. Because they can sing someone's praises or ridicule them in song, griots are both respected and feared.

Griots must also be adept at playing drums and, in some areas, a 21-stringed instrument called the kora, and they must be talented singers. Griots are usually men, but sometimes there are female griots as well. However, female griots (*griottes*) do not travel as widely as their male counterparts, since they are usually tied to their home and the domestic duties of being a wife and mother. Griottes sing a special kind of song called a *saabi*, which is considered subversive because it challenges male authority.

In the past, griots were often the teachers of royal children, the ones who instructed them on their own family history and the traditions and laws of their land. When the chief wished to speak to his village, he whispered to the griot, who then repeated the words loudly enough for everyone to hear. Though griots do not have royal duties anymore, they remain an integral part of their communities.

INTERNET LINKS

allgoodtales.com/storytelling-traditions-across-world-west-africa
Griots in West Africa are the subject of this page.

www.fifa.com/associations/association/BEN
This is the FIFA page for Beninese soccer.

www.responsiblevacation.com/vacations/benin/travel-guide
This travel site offers information about Beninese destinations, arts, and activities.

FESTIVALS

Acrobats perform at the Nokoué Jazz Festival in So-Ava in the Lake Nokoué region.

12

HOLIDAYS AND FESTIVALS IN BENIN reflect the country's ethnic and religious diversity. Public holidays include Christian, Muslim, and Vodun observances. There are also special days for historical and national commemorations, such as Independence Day on August 1.

Christian holidays in Benin include Christmas Day, Easter Sunday and Monday, Whit (Pentecost) Monday, Assumption Day, and All Saints' Day. Muslim holidays are Korité, or Eid al-Fitr, which marks the end of Ramadan; Tabaski, or Eid al-Adha (the Feast of the Sacrifice); and the birthday of the Prophet Muhammad.

Beninese people take part in West African festivals. These fishermen from Benin, Niger, and Nigeria rush to the river in a contest at a fishing festival in Argungu, Nigeria.

A band plays during the Nokoué Jazz Festival, a new music festival created by the Beninese musician Athanase Dehounon.

Traditional festivals often involve costumes and masks, dancing, and music. Among the Yoruba people, Egungun festivals honor the ancestors, and Gelede festivals honor women. These observances are often celebrated with masquerades.

Masquerades are festivals where some people wear costumes to represent something else—an animal, an ancestor, or a spirit. The entire costume, not just the headpiece, is referred to as a mask. The goal of the dancer inside the mask is to convey the wishes of the spirit represented by the costume. This can best be done if the identity of the dancer is unknown. To this end, the dancer often uses a disguised voice when speaking as the spirit. People respect and fear the masks because they are the physical manifestations of the spirits they normally pray to and can bring them good luck, a good harvest, and good fortune, or famine, disease, and death.

Becoming a dancer in a mask is a long and difficult process. Many of the dances that represent the spirits have complicated steps and involve spinning, running, or dancing in difficult rhythms while wearing heavy costumes that are often topped by heavy headgear. Dancers train for years so that they can perform the rituals and dances without disappointing the spirit they represent or the people who look to that spirit for guidance.

EGUNGUN

In orisha worship, *Egungun* is the word for the spirits of the ancestors as a whole. This aspect of the religion assures the dead a place among the living and gives them the responsibility for exhorting the living to uphold traditional standards and ethical mores of past generations. Egungun can provide protection or guidance for the living and can even have the power to punish those who have forgotten about their ancestors. To reveal their messages to the living, the Egungun manifest themselves as masked spirits.

Only those ancestors who are remembered can affect the lives of their descendants. Ancestors who have been forgotten pass on into the realm of the Zamani, where they live with other spirits and gods. Before then, they are in a period called *sasa*, which is the time between the death of their physical body and the death of their memory among the living. When not physically manifested as a masked spirit, ancestors can be invoked at the site of their graves (*ojuorori*), at the family shrine (*ile run*), or in the community grave (*igbale*).

Only men are allowed to connect with the spirits as masked dancers. The mask must cover his entire body so that not even the smallest part of the dancer can be seen. The costume is made of raffia (palm leaves) in some areas, cloth in others. The headdress of the mask is carved from wood or other material, or can be composed of objects such as skulls, antlers, and even gas masks. Besides remaining hidden inside the costume, the dancer must disguise his voice so as to represent the will of the Egungun who speaks through him.

The Egungun can represent either a specific ancestor who has died, all ancestors of a particular family, or even all ancestors generally. Egungun are certain to appear at the annual Egungun festival, the date of which is set by a diviner. The festival can last 7, 14, 17, or 21 days. During this time, people believe that the ancestors return to them to spend some time among their living descendants. Families negotiate for the days when the mask representing their lineage will appear, and on the appointed day, drummers and women of the family sing outside the family compound early in the day. Eventually, the Egungun arrives, stopping first at the graves of the male members of the family, then visiting the homes of family members. The Egungun blesses the family and receives their gifts of gratitude. After this, the Egungun dances through the entire town.

Some masks represent certain spirits. One of these is Egun Bla, which is one of the most feared spirits of the Egungun. Egun Bla symbolizes the dark side of Yoruba religious beliefs. The spirit is offered sacrifices and gifts to appease its vengeful nature. Egun Bla is so powerful that it is believed that hearing it

Masked Egungun dancers sit on a bench, preparing for their performance.

speak would drive a person mad. People do not only fear Egun Bla, however, but they also appeal to it for assistance. A woman who wants to have a child may ask to make a sacrifice before the spirit so that her wish will come true.

When an Egungun dispenses advice, the person is bound to follow through with it. Even though the mask is worn by living persons, it is the dead who are speaking and must be obeyed. It is forbidden for anyone other than the dancer to touch a mask, and some Egungun will chase children, who are terrified to be touched, believing that if the Egungun touches them, they will die. Even adults may be so fearful of the Egungun that a person who is touched by one might faint or collapse. People who have been touched, or even knocked down by an Egungun, believe they have offended the Egungun and will attempt to placate the spirit with a gift of money.

GAANI FESTIVAL

Every year, the Bariba celebrate the La Fête de Gaani ("The Festival of Joy"). This festival celebrates joy, good memories, ethnic solidarity, and Bariba society. An entire month is devoted to finding the funds for the festival. The funds come from villages in the form of money, animals, food, and clothing. Babies, both male and female, born during this month are given the name Gaani before their first name.

When the festival is only a week away, the king invites powerful sorcerers to his palace so that they may cast spells that will protect the celebration and everyone involved. The night before the festival, drums and trumpets are brought out and played all night long.

In the morning on the day of the festival, there is a horse show. In the afternoon, the king and his court emerge from his palace to the music of drums and trumpets and the cheering of the people. They walk for miles to visit sites sacred to the Bariba.

This procession consists of the king and his court followed by musicians. After the musicians come other dignitaries such as the man in charge of the ceremonies and the king's chief poet and genealogist. Behind them come horsemen, and the crowd follows at the end. All told, this procession travels just over 7 miles (12 km) and visits nine sites.

The sacred sites to be visited include Too Yankou Bakararou, where the king says his prayers; Dakirou, where the graves of legendary heroes Bake Doue and his brother Sero Betete are located; and Bankpilou, where the tomb of King Kpe Gounou Kaba Wouko is located.

Once the procession is completed, the king returns to his palace, where he receives the well-wishes of his subjects for another happy and prosperous year.

GELEDE FESTIVAL

The Yoruba Gelede festival occurs between March and May every year. The city of Cové is especially known for its public displays during the period. At this festival, members of the Gelede Society dance to express gratitude for the previous harvest and to invoke the rains for the next plantings. The dance

Just as UNESCO (the United Nations Educational, Scientific and Cultural Organization) works to protect natural and cultural World Heritage sites, it also identifies examples of "intangible cultural heritage of humanity" (ICH) that need to be preserved. These include, according to the group's website, "traditions or living expressions inherited from our ancestors and passed on to our descendants, such as oral traditions, performing arts, social practices, rituals, arts, festive events, knowledge and practices concerning nature and the universe or the knowledge and skills to produce traditional crafts."

The Convention for the Safeguarding of the Intangible Cultural Heritage has listed one entry for Benin, which it shares with Nigeria and Togo—the "Oral Heritage of Gelede." A masked Gelede dancer is shown here.

honors the "Great Mother" of the Yoruba, Iya Nla, who embodies the order inherent in society but who also encompasses a chaotic side. The festival aims to appease or eliminate the negative aspects of Iya Nla and to encourage the beneficial side of her nature.

The masked dancers of the gelede festival dance in time to the beating of drums. The drumbeats come faster and faster until the dancer is a whirling blur. However, the headdress of the costume remains still. This is to embody the Yoruba ideal of summoning peace in a chaotic world. Gelede dancers begin their training when they are five years old.

ZANGBETO MASQUERADE

During the dry season, the Ogu people hold their Zangbeto masquerade. This ceremony is to honor the spirits and is believed to renew the spirituality of the community and the land. This will ensure prosperity and fertility throughout the area. The name of the ceremony comes from the words *zan* ("night") and *beto* ("person"). It is also known as "the Coming Out of the Spirits." The spirits honored were traditionally the ones that protected the kings, the chiefs, and the elders. The Zangbeto masked dancers also act as enforcers of a ruler's authority. They may behave like policemen, maintaining the security of the village at night against bandits. Because people are afraid to be confronted by the masked dancers, they stay in their homes during the night. The dancers sing songs of warning as they enter a village at dusk to remind people to return to their homes. Those who do not obey risk punishment for violating this sacred curfew.

The masks are composed of a raffia costume with a headdress on top, giving them a height of 9 feet (2.7 m) or more. Because of the confining nature of the costume, each masked dancer has a guardian who helps guide him through the village. The dancing rids the village of all evil forces, protecting it until the next dry season, when the masked dancers will emerge from the bush singing their songs and dancing energetically once again.

The Beninese have developed elaborate rituals to help them through the important milestones in their lives such as birth, marriage, and death. Even after death, ancestors continue to visit families in the form of masks and exert influence over the families from the other side. People respect the masks and fear them. Rituals such as marriage and the mask dances bring people together and reinforce their place in the community.

VODUN DAY

Since 1992, Vodun Day (Fête du Vodoun) has been celebrated in Benin on January 10. It's also called Traditional Day, Traditional Religions Day, or Voodoo Day. As a religion, Vodun was suppressed during colonial times and then continued to be repressed under Mathieu Kerekou's regime. However, by 1990, the religion was once again openly practiced, and since 1992, it has been formally recognized.

Former president of Benin Nicephore Soglo claimed Vodun spirits saved his life, and in gratitude, he established Vodun Day. When Kerekou regained

A man dances to the rhythm of drums at a Vodun festival in Allada, Benin.

power, he attempted to abolish the holiday but was unsuccessful. Kerekou himself was the son of a Vodun priestess.

Many of the main festivities occur in Ouidah, where enslaved people were once loaded onto ships at a beach called "the point of no return." Today, people gather on that same beach to play music, dance, pray, and sacrifice animals to the spirits. Other people listen to speeches that praise the religion's positive influence on people's lives. Many people feel the day is not only a festival to remember Vodun but also to remember the untold thousands of Beninese who were taken away in slavery over the centuries.

Although most attendees in Ouidah are from Benin, many people on the beach have traveled from the United States, Brazil, and Haiti. These people have come to discover something about the culture of their ancestors who were enslaved people.

Beninese people from the northern parts of the country bring horses, and, for part of the day, the beach becomes an impromptu racetrack and a place to display one's riding skills. At the end of the day, priests often have feasts at their homes and invite many people to join them, including people who have traveled from other countries to learn about Vodun Day and the religion of their ancestors.

INTERNET LINKS

africaonlinemuseum.org/map/benin/egungun-masks/photos
Colorful images of Egungun masks are presented on this site.

ich.unesco.org/en/RL/oral-heritage-of-gelede-00002
This is the UNESCO Intangible Heritage listing for the Gelede ceremony.

www.officeholidays.com/countries/benin
This calendar site provides a list of holidays in Benin with links to explanations.

www.omenkaonline.com/egungun-festival-yoruba-people
This site provides an overview of Egungun festival practices.

www.wanderlust.co.uk/content/dark-secrets-voodoo-in-benin
This story relates the author's expedition to Benin to experience the Vodun Day Festival.

FOOD

A Beninese woman carries a platter of prepared foods on her head in Porto-Novo.

13

W ITH ITS WIDE DIVERSITY OF ethnic and religious groups, Benin has a wealth of food traditions. Every village has a slightly different style. Common among all is a dependence on fillings, doughy pastes, dumplings, or porridges made of tubers, grains, or beans. These preparations, such as *fufu*, may be very bland in taste and served with sauces or stews, or they can be highly spicy and served alongside fried fish.

EVERYDAY FOODS

In the south, corn is the main staple of everyone's diet. Corn flour is used to make dough, which is cooked and served with sauces made from peanuts or tomatoes. The meats most often eaten are fish and chicken, which are usually fried. Palm or peanut oil is used in frying. Less commonly, people eat goat, rabbit, and even bush rat. Rice, couscous, and beans are eaten quite commonly. In the south, it is usually easy to get fresh fruits such as oranges, bananas, pineapples, and mangoes.

In the north, yams are much more common than corn. Yams are pounded into flour, cooked, and eaten with sauces. Pounding the yams

Kuli-kuli, a snack made from groundnuts, or peanuts, is sometimes called Benin's national dish. After grinding the peanuts and adding spices, the paste is rolled into logs or balls and fried. Kuli-kuli is also popular in Ghana and Nigeria.

Women mash boiled cassava root to make fufu.

into the flour is time-consuming, and sometimes several women will cooperate in the task, taking turns. During the day, one can hear the thunking sound of the women of the village pounding the yam flesh into flour.

As in the south, the sauces that are eaten with the corn or yam dough are often based on tomatoes or peanuts. As the north is not near the ocean, and long-distance travel is not easy, fish is not as common away from the coastal areas. Many northern people make cheese. They also eat rice, couscous, and beans, just as people do in the south. Fruits, especially mangoes, are abundant during certain seasons.

Other popular foods in Benin include *akara*, which are deep-fried balls of black-eye pea mush; and *aloko*, which are spicy fried plantains. A favorite street food is *yovo doko*, a deep-fried sweet fritter, typically topped with powdered sugar.

A cook pan fries some akara over an outdoor fire.

People eat their meals with their fingers. Much of the meal is often in the form of a pasty white substance called fufu. The doughy stuff is made from cassava, plantains, rice, millet, sorghum, or corn, which is boiled and stirred until it is stiff enough to hold its shape. Fufu is eaten by taking small amounts of the carbohydrate-rich food by hand and rolling it into small balls to then dip into a stew, for example. Meat is served in cubes or small pieces, as are cheese, fish, and eggs. This way everything can easily be eaten with the fingers.

At the markets, women sell local delicacies such as bush rat and slugs cooked with onions and hot peppers. These women often station themselves near the places where taxis stop and will wave food under the noses of people just getting out of the taxis to tempt them to try their cooking.

When buying food at the market, the customer does not tell the seller how much food he or she wants but rather how much money they will spend.

YAMS

The yams eaten in Benin are true yams, not the sweet potatoes of American grocery stores, which are sometimes referred to as yams.

Sweet potatoes (Ipomoea batatas) are orange or yellow tubers that taper to a point. They belong to the morning-glory family and are native to the tropics of the Americas. Christopher Columbus brought them to Europe.

Yams (Dioscorea batatas), on the other hand, are not even distantly related to potatoes or sweet potatoes. They were originally cultivated in West Africa around 8000 BCE. The tuber has a dark brown or black skin, which covers off-white, purple, or red flesh inside, depending on the variety. The word yam also comes from West Africa. In past centuries, enslaved Africans who came to America called the sweet potato nyami because it reminded them of the yams of their homeland.

Yams, seen below, can grow to be 7 feet (2.1 m) long and can weigh 120 pounds (50 kg)! Yams must be cooked to remove a substance called dioscorene, which tastes bitter and is mildly toxic to humans. Unlike sweet potatoes, yams are not sweet at all.

The vendor selling the food then doles out however much rice or corn balls would make up that cost and coats them in sauce. Bowls and plates are not disposable; once you use them, you must return them so that the women can clean them and have them ready for the next customer.

A food often served for breakfast is *koko*, a kind of hot cereal made from millet that is strained and eaten with a spoon. If one buys koko at the market, it may be served in a plastic bag. The customer bites a hole in the bag and drinks the koko. At night, it is more common to see a hot dish made from cassava, like tapioca. Roasted peanuts or sugar is often added to this dish.

Some people in Benin make a cheese called *wagasi*. It is made by placing milk into a bowl with a tree sap that helps the milk congeal. This mixture is left out until it turns into cheese. The wagasi is then cut up into cubes and fried before eating.

The cheapest food, which is eaten by the very poor, is a slurry made out of *garri*, or cassava flour. People add water to it and drink the mixture cold. It can also be made into a thick paste like fufu. People who have run out of

A woman sells long plastic bags full of white cassava flour, called *garri*, near Dassa-Zoume, a small city in central Benin.

food before the harvest and have no money eat garri until the harvest comes in. To make garri, people cook cassava tubers into a mash that can be mixed with palm oil. The result is then sieved and dried into a granular form. Garri is similar to fufu, and both are staple dishes in Benin and throughout West Africa, particularly among impoverished people. They are filling and take away hunger but are not very nutritious by themselves. A diet heavily based on these foods is insufficient, particularly for growing children.

TABLE MANNERS

People in Benin always wash their hands before eating, even if washing consists of merely rinsing off their hands in some water. People eat only with their right hands; to eat with the left hand is considered very rude. Talking while eating is also considered rude. Children are warned to be quiet or else they might

A woman enjoys a meal in her pirogue in Ganvie.

choke. They are also taught not to reach for food, that an adult will get it for them. Children often get to eat whatever is left when the adults are finished.

If people walk by, it is considered polite to invite them to eat with you because it is impolite to simply eat in front of others. If you are sharing a taxi, do not be surprised if you are offered part of someone else's snack! In these circumstances, it is polite to say thank you but to refuse to take any.

Everyone in the family eats out of the same bowl. Often, the men eat separately from the women and the children. In families that follow more Western customs, men, women, and children may all eat together.

For celebrations, families will prepare a great deal of food to offer to anyone who comes by. Because people do not have phones, they keep in touch with their families and friends by dressing in their best and then stopping by for a visit on holidays. Visitors are always offered something to eat, even if they are beggars going around the village. For these special occasions, women will prepare salads and bread, which they will rarely serve at any other time.

Hospitality is always taken very seriously, and anyone who comes by will be offered something to eat.

INTERNET LINKS

www.best-country.com/en/africa/benin/food
This site lists some Beninese specialties.

diningforwomen.org/customsandcuisine/customs-and-cuisine-of-benin
This quick overview provides a look at authentic Beninese dishes.

DAHOMEY FISH STEW RECIPE

Red palm oil is available online and lends a distinctive flavor and color. Alternatively, use any cooking oil.

2.5 pounds (1,134 grams) porgy, sea bream, scup, tilapia, or any firm-flesh, low-fat fish filets
flour to dredge fish
salt and black pepper (to taste)
½ cup (120 milliliters) red palm oil (or any cooking oil)
2 onions, finely chopped
2 tomatoes, chopped
1 cup (240 mL) fish stock or water
red pepper flakes or cayenne pepper (to taste)

Cut the fish filets crosswise into 2-inch (5 centimeter) sections. Mix the flour, salt, and pepper in a bowl. Dredge the fish in the flour mixture.

In a skillet, heat the oil over a medium-high heat. Fry the fish in the oil, turning it, just until it is golden brown all over. Do not overcook the fish. Remove the fish, and set aside.

Fry the onions in the skillet until they soften. Add the tomatoes. Stir and cook over medium low heat for about 5 minutes. Add the fish stock (or water). Reduce heat, cover, and simmer for 10 minutes.

Return the fish to the skillet. Add red pepper or small pinch of cayenne to taste. Simmer lightly for 15—20 minutes. Serve with rice.

Serves 4.

DODO OR *ALOKO* (SPICY AFRICAN FRIED PLANTAINS)

This dish is prized in Benin and across West Africa. Other, simpler recipes call for simply frying plain, unspiced plantains or seasoning them with only a little cayenne and salt.

4—6 ripe plantains
¼ medium onion, peeled and cut in pieces
1 teaspoon cayenne or chili pepper
½—1 tablespoon chopped fresh ginger
   (or ¼ teaspoon ground ginger)
1—2 garlic cloves, peeled
1 teaspoon lemon juice
½ teaspoon nutmeg
1 teaspoon salt
oil for deep frying

Cut both ends off the plantains. Use a sharp knife to create a slit in the skin along the length of each plantain, carefully making sure not to cut into the flesh. Remove and discard the skin by peeling it apart. Slice each plantain diagonally into 1-inch (2.5 cm) pieces.

Blend the onion, ginger, garlic, cayenne pepper, lemon juice, nutmeg, and salt in a blender or food processor. If necessary, add just enough water to facilitate blending.

In a large bowl, toss the plantain slices with the ginger spice mixture. Let the coated plantain rest for about 10—20 minutes to absorb the flavor.

Heat up a large skillet or cast iron pan with oil up to 0.5 inch (1.27 cm) deep over a medium-high heat until it is hot but not smoking. Fry the plantain pieces in batches, turning once, until golden brown, about 5 minutes. Do not overcrowd the pan or the plantains will be soggy. Using a slotted spoon, transfer the fried plantains to a platter lined with paper towels.

Serve warm as a snack (in Benin, they are often served with peanuts), or alongside fried fish or black-eyed pea porridge as a meal.

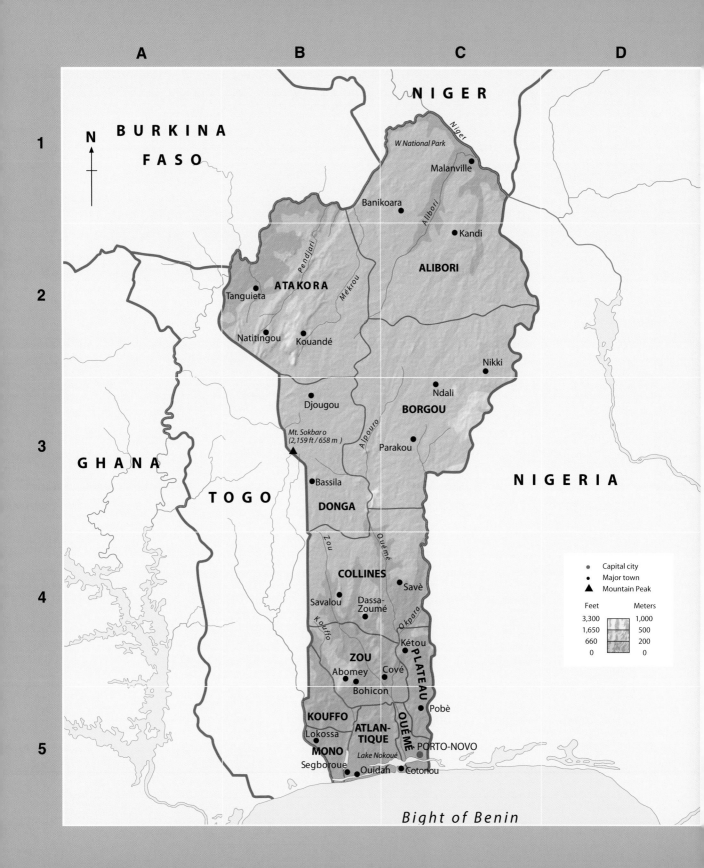

MAP OF BENIN

Abomey, B4
Alibori River, B1, B2, C1, C2
Alpouro River, B3, C3, C2
Atakora, B1, B2
Atlantique, B5, C5

Banikoara, C1
Bassila, B3
Bight of Benin, B5, C5
Bohicon, B4
Borgou, B2, B3, C2, C3

Collines, B3, B4, C3, C4
Cotonou, C5
Cové, C4

Dassa-Zoumé, B4
Djougou, B3
Donga, B3, B4

Ghana, A2—A5, B5

Kandi, C2
Kétou, C4
Kouandé, B2
Kouffo, B4, B5
Kouffo River, B4

Lake Nokoué, B5, C5
Lokossa, B5

Malanville, C1
Mékrou River, B1, B2
Mono, B5
Mt. Sokbaro, B3

Natitingou, B2
Ndali, C3
Nikki, C2

Okpara River, C4
Ouémé, C5
Ouémé River, B4, C4
Ouidah, B5

Parakou, C3
Pendjari River, B1, B2
Plateau, C4, C5
Pobè, C5
Porto-Novo, C5

Savalou, B4
Savè, C4
Segboroue, B5

Tanguieta, B2

W National Park, C1

Zou, B4, B5, C4, C5
Zou River, B4, C5

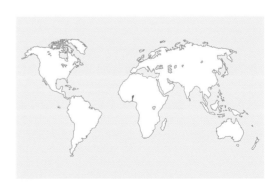

ECONOMIC BENIN

Agriculture

- Cassava and peanuts
- Corn
- Cotton
- Palm Fruit

Services

- Hydroelectricity
- Tourism

Natural Resources

- Fish
- Gold
- Iron
- Phosphates

ABOUT THE ECONOMY

All figures are 2017 estimates unless otherwise noted.

GROSS DOMESTIC PRODUCT (GDP OFFICIAL EXCHANGE RATE)
$9.246 billion

GDP PER CAPITA
$2,300

GDP BY SECTOR
agriculture: 26.1 percent
industry: 22.8 percent
services: 51.1 percent

POPULATION BELOW POVERTY LINE
36.2 percent (2011)

CURRENCY
West African CFA franc (XOF)
US$1 = $558.18 XOF (October 2020)
coins: 1, 5, 10, 25, 50, 100, 250, 500 francs
notes: 500, 1,000, 2,000, 5,000, 10,000 francs

AGRICULTURAL PRODUCTS
cotton, corn, cassava (manioc, tapioca), yams, beans, palm oil, peanuts, cashews; livestock

INDUSTRIAL PRODUCTS
textiles, food processing, construction materials, cement

MAJOR EXPORTS
cotton, cashews, shea butter, textiles, palm products, seafood

MAJOR IMPORTS
foodstuffs, capital goods, petroleum products

TOURISM
295,000 annual tourists (2018)

MAJOR TRADE PARTNERS
exports:
Bangladesh, India, Ukraine, Niger, China, Nigeria, Turkey

imports:
Thailand, India, France, China, Togo, Netherlands, Belgium

CULTURAL BENIN

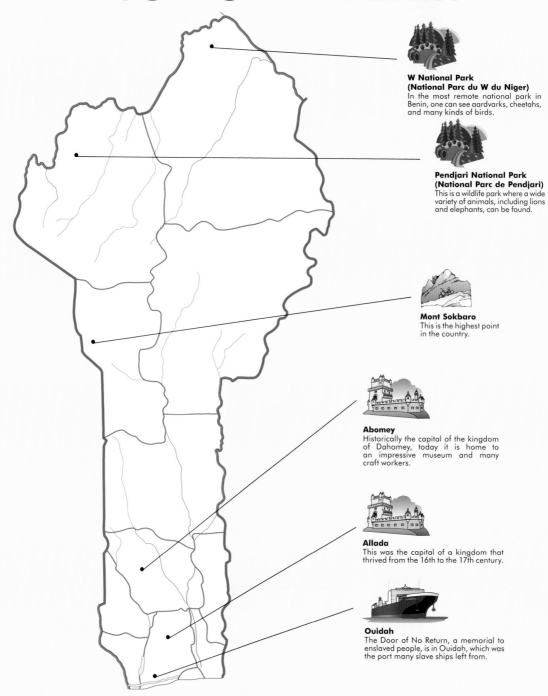

**W National Park
(National Parc du W du Niger)**
In the most remote national park in Benin, one can see aardvarks, cheetahs, and many kinds of birds.

**Pendjari National Park
(National Parc de Pendjari)**
This is a wildlife park where a wide variety of animals, including lions and elephants, can be found.

Mont Sokbaro
This is the highest point in the country.

Abomey
Historically the capital of the kingdom of Dahomey, today it is home to an impressive museum and many craft workers.

Allada
This was the capital of a kingdom that thrived from the 16th to the 17th century.

Ouidah
The Door of No Return, a memorial to enslaved people, is in Ouidah, which was the port many slave ships left from.

ABOUT THE CULTURE

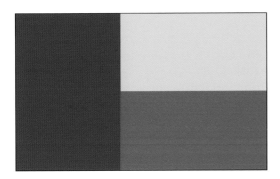

All figures are 2020 estimates unless otherwise noted.

COUNTRY NAME
Republic of Benin

CAPITAL
Porto-Novo is the official capital, but the seat of government is in Cotonou.

OTHER MAJOR CITIES
Ouidah, Parakou, Djougou, Abomey

STATE FLAG
two equal horizontal bands of yellow (on top) and red, with a vertical green band on the hoist side

POPULATION
12,864,634

ETHNIC GROUPS
Fon and related 38.4 percent, Adja and related 15.1 percent, Yoruba and related 12 percent, Bariba and related 9.6 percent, Fulani and related 8.6 percent, Ottamari and related 6.1 percent, Yoa-Lokpa and related 4.3 percent, Dendi and related 2.9 percent, other 0.9 percent, foreigner 1.9 percent (2013)

LIFE EXPECTANCY AT BIRTH
total population: 61.4 years
male: 59.6 years
female: 63.3 years

RELIGIONS
Muslim 27.7 percent, Roman Catholic 25.5 percent, Protestant 13.5 percent (Celestial 6.7 percent, Methodist 3.4 percent, other Protestant 3.4 percent), Vodun 11.6 percent, other Christian 9.5 percent, other traditional religions 2.6 percent, other 2.6 percent, none 5.8 percent (2013)

OFFICIAL LANGUAGE
French (official), Fon and Yoruba (most common vernaculars in south), tribal languages (at least six major ones in north)

LITERACY RATE
total population: 42.4 percent
male: 54 percent
female: 31.1 percent (2018)

TIMELINE

IN BENIN	IN THE WORLD
1620	**1620**
The Kingdom of Dahomey is founded.	Pilgrims sail the *Mayflower* to America.
1730	
Dahomey becomes a tributary state of the Yoruba kingdom of Oyo.	**1776**
	The U.S. Declaration of Independence is written.
	1789–1799
1818	The French Revolution takes place.
Dahomey shakes off Oyo overlordship under King Ghezo.	**1861**
1892–1894	The American Civil War begins.
War with the French breaks out.	
1894	
King Behanzin is deposed; France installs a puppet king.	
1904	
Dahomey becomes a French colony.	**1914**
	World War I begins.
	1939–1945
1946	World War II devastates Europe.
Dahomey becomes an overseas territory of France.	**1957**
	The Russians launch *Sputnik*.
1960	
Dahomey becomes independent of France.	
1963	
The first major government collapse occurs.	
1965	
The government collapses; Christophe Soglo is installed in power.	**1966–1969**
	The Chinese Cultural Revolution takes place.
1967	
Soglo is replaced by Maurice Kouandete.	
1968	
A new government is established by Emile Zinsou.	**1969**
	U.S. astronaut Neil Armstrong becomes the first human on the moon.
1972	
Mathieu Kerekou begins his socialist policies.	
1975	
The country's name is changed from Dahomey to People's Republic of Benin.	

IN BENIN	IN THE WORLD
1985	
Students demonstrate against Kerekou.	**1986**
1990	A nuclear power disaster occurs
A new constitution is ratified, and	at Chernobyl in Ukraine.
the country becomes a democracy.	
1991	**1991**
Nicephore Soglo is elected president.	The Soviet Union breaks up.
1992	
Benin legalizes Vodun Day as a national	
holiday, to take place every January 10.	
1996	
Kerekou is elected president.	**1997**
1999	Britain returns Hong Kong to China.
The country's 6 provinces are	
divided into 12 departments.	
2001	**2001**
Kerekou is reelected president.	Terrorists attack the United States on September 11.
2003	**2003**
National Assembly elections are held.	The Iraq War begins.
2006	
Thomas Boni Yayi is elected president.	**2008**
2009	Americans elect their first African
Benin announces discovery of oil	American president, Barack Obama.
offshore near the Nigeria-Benin border.	
2016	**2015–2016**
Businessman Patrice Talon is elected president.	ISIS launches terror attacks in Belgium and France.
	2017
	Donald Trump becomes U.S. president.
	Hurricane Maria devastates Caribbean
	islands and Puerto Rico.
2019	**2019**
Low turnout for parliamentary elections; all	Notre Dame Cathedral in Paris is damaged by fire.
opposition parties are banned from running.	**2020**
2021	COVID-19 pandemic spreads around the world.
The next presidential election is scheduled.	Joe Biden wins U.S. presidential election.

GLOSSARY

asooke
Traditional Yoruba cloths made by men, including *etu*, *sanyan*, and *alaari*.

aze
Bad magic that harms people.

babalao
A Yoruba diviner.

bata
A Yoruba drum ensemble.

bo
Good magic that aids people.

bokono
A Fon diviner.

Egungun
Yoruba term for the spirits of the ancestors as a whole.

fa
In Vodun, a person's destiny.

griot
A traditional storyteller and historian; a keeper of oral traditions.

houngan
A male Vodun priest.

kijipa
A traditional indigo-and-white striped Yoruba cloth woven by women.

kpojito
The reign-mate of the king of Dahomey, a woman always chosen from the common people.

manbo
A female Vodun priest.

ori
In orisha worship, a person's destiny.

orisha worship
The native religion of the Yoruba.

Vodun
The West African traditional religion of the Fon people of Benin, also called vodou or voodoo.

FOR FURTHER INFORMATION

BOOKS

Alpern, Stanley B. *Amazons of Black Sparta, 2nd Edition: The Women Warriors of Dahomey.* New York, NY: New York University Press, 2011.

Butler, Stuart. *Benin.* Chalfont St. Peter, UK: Bradt Travel Guides, 2019.

Eltis, David, and David Richardson. *Atlas of the Transatlantic Slave Trade.* New Haven, CT: Yale University Press, 2015.

Lonely Planet. *West Africa.* Franklin, TN: Lonely Planet Global, Inc., 2017.

Mama, Raouf. *Fortune's Favored Child.* Evanston, IL: Curbstone Books, Northwest University Press, 2014.

Mama, Raouf. *Why Monkeys Live in Trees.* Evanston,IL: Curbstone Books, Northwest University Press, 2006.

UNESCO. *The Women Soldiers of Dahomey.* Glasgow, UK: Collins (UNESCO Publishing), 2016.

ONLINE

BBC News. "Benin Country Profile." www.bbc.com/news/world-africa-13037572.

Britannica. "Benin." www.britannica.com/place/Benin.

CIA. *The World Factbook.* "Benin." www.cia.gov/library/publications/the-world-factbook/geos/bn.html.

UNESCO World Heritage. "Benin." whc.unesco.org/en/statesparties/bj.

World Atlas. "Maps of Benin." www.worldatlas.com/maps/benin.

MUSIC

Angelique Kidjo. *Remain in Light.* Kravenworks, 2018.

Marcos Branda Lacerda. *The World's Musical Traditions 8: Yoruba Drums from Benin, West Africa.* Smithsonian Folkways Recordings, 1996.

Niger/Northern Benin: Music of the Fulani. UNESCO, 2015.

Various artists. *Benin: Bariba Music.* OUTHERE, 2013.

VIDEOS

Dicing With Death. Episode 3: "Benin: Cotton at All Costs." Tony Comiti Productions, 2013.

In Search of Voodoo: Roots to Heaven. FilmBuff, 2019.

Laduma: Benin's Journey. Shami Media Group, 2016.

World Music Portraits: Angelique Kidjo. Shanachie, 2003.

BIBLIOGRAPHY

Al Jazeera. Benin archives. www.aljazeera.com/where/benin.

BBC News. "Benin Country Profile." www.bbc.com/news/world-africa-13037572.

CIA. *The World Factbook*. "Benin." https://www.cia.gov/library/publications/the-world-factbook/geos/print_bn.html.

Croitoru, Lelia, Juan Jose Miranda, and Maria Sarraf. "The Cost of Coastal Zone Degradation in West Africa: Benin, Côte d'Ivoire, Senegal and Togo." West Africa Coastal Areas Management Program, World Bank Group. March 2019. documents1.worldbank.org/curated/en/822421552504665834/pdf/The-Cost-of-Coastal-Zone-Degradation-in-West-Africa-Benin-Cote-dIvoire-Senegal-and-Togo.pdf.

Constitute. "Benin's Constitution of 1990." Constituteproject.org. www.constituteproject.org/constitution/Benin_1990.pdf?lang=en.

Global Nature Fund. "Manatee Protection and Mangrove Conservation in West Africa." www.globalnature.org/en/manatees-mangroves-benin.

Humanium. "Children of Benin." April 11, 2020. www.humanium.org/en/benin.

Humanium. "Forced Marriage in Benin." June 27, 2018. www.humanium.org/en/forced-marriage-in-benin.

Misachi, John. "Ganvie, Benin—Unique Places Around the World." *World Atlas Travel*, August 3, 2017. https://www.worldatlas.com/articles/ganvie-benin-unique-places-around-the-world.html.

Nir, Sarah Maslin. "It Was a Robust Democracy. Then the New President Took Power." *New York Times,* July 4, 2019. www.nytimes.com/2019/07/04/world/africa/benin-protests-talon-yayi.html.

Okanla, Karim. "Strained Relations." D+C Development and Cooperation, March 28, 2020. www.dandc.eu/en/article/petrol-smuggling-has-had-negative-impact-benins-relations-its-giant-neighbour-nigeria.

Orjinmo, Nduka. "Nigeria's Border Crisis Fuelled by Rice." *BBC News*, October 31, 2019. www.bbc.com/news/world-africa-50223045.

Pan African Visions. "Benin: U.S. Lawmaker Says President Patrice Talon of Benin Has Not Preserved the Gift He Was Given..." October 1, 2020. panafricanvisions.com/2020/10/beninu-s-lawmaker-says-president-patrice-talon-of-benin-has-not-preserved-the-gift-he-was-given.

Russonello, Giovanni. "It's Angélique Kidjo's Birthday, and Her Country's Too." *New York Times,* March 14, 2020. www.nytimes.com/2020/03/12/arts/music/angelique-kidjo-carnegie-hall.html.

UNESCO World Heritage. "Benin." whc.unesco.org/en/statesparties/bj.

WHO in Africa. "Benin." www.afro.who.int/fr/countries/benin.

World Bank Group. "Benin." www.worldbank.org/en/country/benin/overview.

INDEX

INDEX